THE FLAVOUR-LED WEANING COOKBOOK

THE FLAVOUR-LED WEANING COOKBOOK

Easy recipes & meal plans to wean happy, healthy, adventurous eaters

~~~

ZAINAB JAGOT AHMED

EBURY
PRESS

I love my daughter Aaliyah. She ignites a creativity in me I wasn't even aware I had until after her birth. Her 'needs' have become my 'needs', and her infectious happiness has become my happiness – I wouldn't have it any other way! My little angel is the inspiration behind my cookbooks and she makes me a better mum, who's always keen to provide her with a well-balanced, nutrient-rich diet, tasty home-cooked meals and the best start in life. This book is for you, Aaliyah.

CONTENTS

INTRODUCTION

My daughter is five years old now. When we started our weaning journey I read numerous weaning books, websites, blogs and forums to learn as much as I could about weaning techniques. But the recipes that went along with the expert guidance left me uninspired. The purees, first finger foods and first meals were bland and boring and, frankly, a million miles away from meals I cooked at home. It seemed strange, to me, to wean my daughter with meals that were completely unlike what I would be feeding her in the future. Surely I would have a battle on my hands when I transitioned Aaliyah over to our family meals?

I set about inventing weaning recipes that followed all of the expert guidance regarding safety and nutrition, but also incorporated lots of baby-friendly flavours. I wanted Aaliyah's first foods to be fun and delicious. I wanted her to love food, and to love a variety of flavours.

Every meal I created was followed by the 'taste test'. I wouldn't feed Aaliyah a meal I wasn't prepared to eat myself. If it tasted good to me, considering it had no added salt or sugar in it, I offered it to her. And my method worked!

My culinary heritage revolves around Asian cuisine so this was my starting point: the flavours I knew and loved best. Many of the recipes I devised became my first book, *Easy Indian SuperMeals*.

I didn't feed my daughter only Indian flavours, though. I introduced her to a broad range of flavours to keep mealtimes fun. So, here, I want to show you how you can entice your baby with an array of baby-safe flavours inspired by cuisines from all over the world.

This book contains all of my research into nutritional requirements, food groups and the potential health benefits of herbs and spices. I have included over 100 new, tried-and-tested flavour-packed recipes for every stage of the weaning process that your baby will love. Use this cookbook in conjunction with the latest government guidelines on weaning, and your little one will receive a well-balanced diet and develop lots of happy little taste buds and a healthy, broad palate.

Aaliyah is an excellent eater these days. She's always willing to try new meals, which makes my life easier when it comes to ensuring she's munching all the vitamins and minerals she needs for healthy growth. It's very satisfying to see your little one enjoy the meals you have prepared, but equally it can be frustrating when meals are rejected. Try to relax and be prepared to offer the same meal to your little one many times before the taste and flavour is accepted.

THE CULINARY ADVENTURE BEGINS!

Weaning is a huge milestone for baby and usually takes place around 6 months, when baby begins to show her parents signs that she is ready to take on the world of solid food, and no longer needs to be exclusively reliant on breast milk or formula for her nutrients.

Breast milk or formula is still very much a part of a baby's diet up until the age of 12 months (and sometimes beyond this age). During weaning, solid food and your baby's usual milk will work alongside each other.

Guidelines advocate that all babies be exclusively breast-fed or formula-fed until 6 months of age. Then parents can begin weaning their baby from around 6 months. However, in reality this may not always be possible. And some parents may choose to begin weaning their little one from as early as 17 weeks (4 months).

I waited until Aaliyah was 6 months old before starting her weaning journey and there are a number of reasons why I think it's a good idea to hold off.

WHY WAIT UNTIL 6 MONTHS?

* **Digestive system and allergic reactions:** Waiting until around 6 months ensures your little one's digestive system is ready for solid food, reducing the chances of allergic reactions occurring. Common allergy symptoms include tummy upsets, skin rashes, swelling of the lips and face, runny and blocked noses, sneezing, itchy watery eyes, nausea, vomiting and diarrhoea. See more on how to watch for allergies on page 19.
* **Nature says 'No':** A baby's tongue-thrust reflex, which means she pushes food out of her mouth with her tongue, is present

until babies are 4–6 months (at least 17 weeks), and is nature's way of telling us baby is not yet ready for solid food. Equally, baby needs time to refine her motor skills, so she can move food around inside her mouth and swallow it, instead of pushing it out. Weaning will be quicker and less messy when she is ready.

∗ **Baby's milk is a 'complete food':** Research shows that breast milk or formula is a 'complete food' for a baby, providing her with all the nutrients she needs until she is 6 months, at which point she should start to receive some nutrients through food – iron in particular.

∗ **Antibody protection:** A mother's breast milk contains antibodies to naturally protect baby against infections. So breastfeeding exclusively until 6 months helps to ensure your little one is protected, and will continue to protect her for as long as you choose to breastfeed her.

If you do choose to wean your little one earlier, you'll hear no judgement from me! Weaning is very much an individual process. Babies are little people ready for milestones at different times. Yes, we have an idea of when this milestone will happen, but it doesn't happen at exactly the same time for each baby. So if you feel baby is ready for solids earlier than 6 months, it's best to have a chat with your health visitor first.

While there is some flexibility around when to start weaning a baby, healthcare professionals are all united on one thing: babies SHOULD NOT be weaned earlier than 4 months (17 weeks). Their digestive systems simply aren't ready for solid food.

SIGNALS THAT BABY IS READY FOR WEANING

* Baby can sit up straight and hold her head steady.
* Baby's eye, hand and mouth movements are more co-ordinated. She can focus on food, pick it up with her fingers and put it in her mouth.
* Her tongue-thrust reflex has gone and she can swallow food. You should wait until your baby exhibits these three signs together before you begin weaning your little one.

FREQUENT FAKE 'READY FOR WEANING' SIGNALS

Some signals are commonly mistaken as 'ready for weaning' signals. A major culprit behind this confusion is a growth spurt.

Babies experience many growth spurts throughout their first year – many parents feel their babies have one at roughly 4 months of age. These growth spurts will make your baby hungrier and likely wanting more milk feeds. But don't be fooled, these symptoms usually pass quite quickly (although they can last for up to a week or two). Aaliyah's first growth spurt lasted around three days and it was hard work! It did make me contemplate introducing solid food early. But I decided to ride it out and stuck with my plan to begin weaning from 6 months.

Equally, growth spurts seem to make your little one restless so she may wake more than normal during the night. Again, this is not a sign baby is not getting enough sustenance through milk alone. The growth spurt will pass and normality will return, at which point you'll no longer feel like a walking zombie, falling asleep virtually anywhere.

A baby devouring her fist is not a sign she is ready for solid food, since everything goes into the mouth. A baby's sense of touch hasn't developed yet so this is her way of discovering the new world she lives in. It is not a sign she is hungry for solids.

WEANING TECHNIQUES

There are two main techniques commonly used when weaning a baby – spoon feeding and baby-led weaning. Here is a quick overview:

SPOON FEEDING (SPOON-LED WEANING)

Spoon feeding is when you begin by feeding your baby pureed, runny food from a spoon – it's that simple! It's best to use a soft-tipped weaning spoon. These are gentle on your little one's gums and are shallow, ensuring you don't over-fill the spoon.

In the early stages of weaning more food will end up on the floor, on your little one's face and over her tray than in her mouth, and there is no need for concern. Initially weaning is about the experience, getting your little one used to the idea of eating solid food, rather than the amount she consumes. She'll still be getting most of her nutrients from milk. As time goes on, you can increase the amount of solid food you are offering.

If you begin weaning earlier than 6 months, you will need to spoon feed her as your little one will be unable to co-ordinate her movements and will require some assistance. From 6–7 months you can either spoon feed or you can opt to use the baby-led weaning technique (see below) with simple finger foods.

At some point your little one may reject eating from a spoon altogether so you might adopt baby-led weaning during your little one's weaning journey.

BABY-LED WEANING

Baby-led weaning is a technique adopted from the age of 6–7 months (no earlier) when baby has usually developed the ability to co-ordinate her movements – hands, eyes and mouth – so she can feed herself. It's simply an opportunity to take advantage of baby's natural grasping reflex, so in addition to toys and rattles going towards her little mouth, food will be too.

If you try baby-led weaning, you need to be very careful when your little one is feeding herself. Finger foods (and even soft purees) are a choking hazard so you must be in the room supervising at all times as your baby eats.

It's also important to feed your little one finger foods suitable for her age range only. In addition, finger foods should be soft, melt-in-the-mouth and either stick shaped or cut into bite-size pieces (see page 126). If you try baby-led weaning, and when you introduce finger foods, it's good to be flexible and offer a little help when your baby needs it. And see a health professional if you are concerned about your baby's intake.

WHICH TECHNIQUE IS BETTER?

There really is no right or wrong answer. Some parents kick off with spoon feeding, then introduce baby-led weaning, or use a combination of both. Other parents bypass purees and head straight for the baby-led weaning approach. This is quite common amongst parents who have successfully weaned their first child so are more confident with their second or third baby. If you are heading straight for the finger foods, you can find my tips and recipes from page 126 onwards.

I must admit, Aaliyah never rejected the spoon. She was quite happy to sit back, relax and let Mummy do all the work. All she had to do was open her mouth and wait for the yummy food to come to her. That said, I did incorporate baby-led weaning (finger foods) into her weaning journey as well, from 7 months. She was quite happy to eat and 'play' with them at snack times, sometimes even choosing to decorate the floor with them! At main mealtimes however, I would spoon feed her.

Aaliyah LOVED eating blueberries as a snack. I cut them into small pieces to make sure they were safe, and gave them to her. She'd pop them in her mouth and roll them around like yummy jelly sweets. When she was old enough, she also loved roti (chapatti) as a snack. She'd suck on the little pieces until they were completely soaked through, and then she'd finish the job.

WHAT IS FLAVOUR-LED WEANING?

The objective of flavour-led weaning is to prepare baby for the big table by using flavours that reflect your personal home cooking. Home cooking varies from home to home, culture to culture. It's what makes us all unique, and our food so yummy! The key to flavour-led weaning is to incorporate as many of these flavours into your little one's diet as possible, whether you are following a spoon-fed or baby-led weaning method. And as baby grows, you can develop her palate further by introducing herbs and spices.

THE FLAVOUR-LED WEANING FLOWER

Imagine the stem of a flower with a closed flower bud at the top. The stem represents basic first tastes (around 6 months/at least 17 weeks). After first tastes and simple mixed ingredient purees have been accepted, and your baby is at least 6 months old, you can get creative by adding herbs and spices to your baby's meals. This is when the flower bud (your little one's taste buds) will begin to open and blossom. The more you nurture your little one's taste buds by offering delicious flavours – bitter, sour, sweet and savoury – the more her taste buds will open and flourish, and the more diverse her palate will become. In my experience, there are many benefits to encouraging a diverse flavour palate for baby:

* Baby will develop a positive relationship with food, excited to try tasty new meals
* It reduces the chance of fussy-eating behaviours emerging
* Natural flavour enhancers may contribute added health benefits
* As your baby's diet becomes more reliant on solid food it will be less challenging for you to help her achieve a well-balanced diet, if she is accepting of new foods
* A broad and balanced diet is essential to make sure that your baby is receiving all of the vitamins and minerals required for healthy growth.

THE FLAVOUR-LED WEANING FLOWER

Flavour-led Weaning Objective: 'To prepare baby for the big table using realistic flavours - flavours reflective of your personal home cooking'

GROWN-UPS

Big family meals

12 MONTHS

Chunkier meals and new flavour-blends

11 MONTHS

10 MONTHS

Introducing flavour-blends and texture

9 MONTHS

8 MONTHS

7 MONTHS

Mixed ingredient purees with single flavour

6 MONTHS

First tastes & mixed ingredient purees

5 MONTHS

4 MONTHS

FLAVOUR-LED WEANING

BABY-LED WEANING

SPOON FEEDING

WHEN DOES FLAVOUR-LED WEANING BEGIN?

This is not a substitute for spoon-led and baby-led weaning but rather a way to ensure your baby transitions well to solids and develops a healthy love of many foods at the same time, reducing the hard work later on. So spoon-led and baby-led weaning are the 'root' for weaning. You should choose which method works best for your baby. Flavour-led weaning recipes work alongside either weaning method to help your baby's palate flourish into a beautiful, colourful, fragrant flower.

Flavour-led weaning starts from the moment your little one is ready for first tastes – single ingredient purees (from around 6 months/at least 17 weeks). Every new fruit or vegetable baby tries is important for her palate. But don't linger on a few tastes: flavour-led weaning is about developing little taste buds so food is always interesting. This is why enhancing the taste of food with herbs and spices (from 6 months) is important. If your little one's palate doesn't progress, food will become uninteresting.

Tailor your baby's flavour-led weaning journey using this book for guidance and inspiration. Wean your baby with flavours close to your culinary heritage for a seamless transition to your family's meals when baby is 12 months. Or, simply, to keep your little one's palate as broad as possible. See pages 20–1 for an overview of all the herbs and spices used in this cookbook and page 213 for further flavour inspiration by cuisine.

ALTERNATIVES TO SALT AND SUGAR

Herbs and spices are excellent alternatives to adding salt and sugar to meals to make them tasty. The delectable aromas that herbs and spices release when they are cooked encourage baby to eat and offer layers of flavour for her to experience. Baby gets maximum yummy flavour while avoiding salt and sugar.

THE FLAVOUR-LED WEANING PLAN

A baby's taste buds first start to develop inside the womb and, after birth, baby has tens of thousands of tiny little taste buds sitting on her tongue. With so many taste buds each new flavour will be a BIG sensory firework for baby, so you need to take it slow when introducing new tastes. Remember, baby has never tried food before!

Flavour-led weaning follows the 4 recommended weaning stages, which can begin from around 6 months and no earlier than 17 weeks, depending on your baby.

STAGE 1	Purees from about 6 months (and at least 17 weeks)
STAGE 2	Flavour blends and textures (7–9 months)
STAGE 3	Chunkier meals and new flavour blends (10–12 months)
STAGE 4	Big table meals (12 months+)

NB: If you are baby-led weaning, you can introduce soft finger foods from 6 months, as long as your baby is ready.

In this book, during **stage 1**, I suggest 3 simple phases to introduce flavours quickly and safely:

1. Start with **Foundation Flavours**: these are simple, single ingredient purees made from veg and fruit.

2. After 2 weeks, or when your baby is ready, start on **Mixed Ingredient Flavours**, which combine two to three ingredients in puree form.

3. As a final phase, introduce baby-friendly herbs and spices with some **Flavour Switches**.

Begin weaning by keeping it simple: start with single ingredient purees. After first tastes have been accepted crack on to the next phase. Then continue to develop your little one's taste buds gradually, one stage at a time, as I outline in this book.

THE FLAVOUR: HERBS AND SPICES

There are many different herbs and spices suitable for weaning, but they must be 100% natural. Available in fresh, ground or dried varieties, most are safe to use as long as your baby isn't allergic to them (see opposite for allergy symptoms). Start with just a little and build up from there.

Pinning down the flavours of herbs and spices can be tricky – there are many levels of depth (for example, cinnamon tastes sweet, but has woody and warm undertones), making just one herb or spice a culinary adventure for your little one. So follow my 'flavour-switch feeding plan' recipes on page 64 for safe introduction and quick transition. Turn to pages 20 and 21 for a guide to baby-friendly herbs and spices suitable from 6 months+.

SPICE ADVICE

Spices are available in whole and ground varieties. You can also buy spices whole and use a pestle and mortar to grind them into a powder as required.

All spices you buy must be produced by reputable brands and sealed with a clear expiry date on the packet. If you are unfamiliar with spice brands, buy them from well-known supermarkets only. Once the packet is opened, store the spices in a clean, dry, airtight container away from sunlight, to ensure spices remain fresh for your baby.

BEING CAUTIOUS – TESTING FOR ALLERGIES

To be cautious, or if you have a known family history of allergies, I would recommend waiting 2–3 days after you introduce one spice to your little one's diet before you introduce another. Up to 72 hours should be more than enough time for you to spot any allergic reactions baby might have to a certain spice. While allergic reactions to spices are uncommon, they can occur. So keep an eye out for tummy upsets, skin rashes, swelling of the lips and face, runny and blocked noses, sneezing, itchy watery eyes, nausea, vomiting and diarrhoea. If in doubt, or there is a family history of allergies to spices, please consult with your doctor or health visitor.

FIRST SPICES AND HERBS FOR BABY

The sweet spices and herbs below are great to start with: sweet, woody, floral flavours really lift the taste of purees. Cinnamon, vanilla and basil were particular favourites of Aaliyah's.

* Basil
* Cardamom
* Cinnamon
* Cloves
* Nutmeg
* Ginger
* Vanilla (not essence or extract)
* Saffron

Some great first savoury flavours to try include:

* Black pepper
* Chives
* Coriander
* Cumin
* Dill
* Garlic Powder
* Mint
* Oregano
* Parsley
* Rosemary
* Turmeric

These all offer peppery, earthy, citrusy and smoky undertones, and are a great contrast to sweet herbs and spices.

SINGLE FLAVOURS

Allspice (ground) Earthy, sweet	Star anise Liquorice, sweet, aniseed	Basil Peppery, sweet anise	Bay leaves Bitter
Black pepper Peppery, earthy	Cardamom Sweet	Chives Mild oniony	Cinnamon Sweet, earthy, warm
Cloves Sweet, earthy	Coriander (ground) Earthy, peppery	Cumin (ground) Smoky, earthy	Dill Sweet, citrusy, bitter
Fennel (seeds) Liquorice, sweet, aniseed	Garlic powder Savoury, caramely	Ginger (ground and fresh) Sweet, warm, woody	Marjoram Oregano(ish) but slightly sweeter
Mint Cool, fresh, hint of sweet	Nutmeg Nutty, sweet, warm	Oregano Earthy, spicy undertones	Paprika (mild) Sweet, warm
Parsley Bitter, lemony	Rosemary Earthy, piny	Saffron Floral	Sage Bitter, woody, warm
Thyme Earthy	Turmeric Bitter, peppery	Vanilla Sweet	White pepper Hot, peppery
Red chilli powder Tangy, hot	Cayenne pepper Hot	Hot paprika Smoky, hot	Crushed chilli flakes Fiery
Mustard seeds Fiery, nutty	Coriander leaf Citrusy	Lemongrass Citrusy	

SUPERMARKET BLENDS

Tandoori masala BBQ(ish)	Mild curry powder Deep, earthy, hint of sweet	Hot curry powder Deep, earthy, hot	Garam masala Aromatic
Italian mixed herbs Aromatic, citrusy, herby	Jerk seasoning* Hot, spicy	Herbes de Provence Mild, herby	Mixed spice Sweet, warm

Pink – 6 months+

Blue – 7 months+

Orange – 10 months+

Yellow – 3 years+

Green – 5 years+

*If Jerk seasoning blend is homemade without chilli powder, it can be offered from 10 months

Spice blends are best introduced after 10 months as they are usually a combination of at least five spices or more, which may overwhelm a 7-month-old's taste buds. Always check the label on supermarket blends to avoid added salt.

BALANCE

A balanced diet is essential. It provides your little one with vital vitamins and minerals required for her tiny body to grow, develop and function effectively – maintaining and repairing muscles, blood vessels, bones and internal organs. A diet lacking in the right balance can lead to growth and developmental problems.

A well-balanced diet can be achieved through eating a wide range of foods from five main food groups: **Starchy Foods, Fruit and Vegetables, Dairy, Protein-rich Foods and Healthy Fats**. All food groups have their own mix of vitamins and minerals. Found in tiny amounts they all play a big role in helping to ensure good health, growth and development.

Below are examples of foods included in each food group:

* **Starchy foods:** bread, rice, potatoes, pasta, fortified breakfast cereals, rice, chapattis, pitta bread, couscous and plantains.
* **Fruit and vegetables (by colour)**
Red and pink: cherries, red grapes, guava, papaya, raspberries, red peppers, strawberries, tomatoes, watermelon.
Yellow and orange: apricots, cantaloupe melons, carrots, lemons, mangoes, oranges, peaches, pumpkins, squash, sweet potatoes.
Green: asparagus, avocados, broccoli, cabbage, kale, lettuce, peas, spinach, watercress.
Blue and purple: aubergine, beetroots, blackberries, blueberries, black grapes, plums, prunes, raisins, raspberries.
White: apples, bananas, cauliflower, mushrooms, onions.
* **Dairy:** milk, cheese, yogurt, fromage frais and custard.
* **Protein-rich Foods:** lean red meat, poultry, fish, eggs, nuts and pulses (e.g. beans, lentils and peas), and foods made from pulses (e.g. tofu and other soya products, hummus).
* **Healthy Fats:** breastmilk, formula, oily fish (e.g. salmon, sardines), nuts and vegetable oils (e.g. rapeseed and olive).

VITAMINS AND MINERALS: THE BIG 9!

Below is an outline of how these key vitamins are vital for your baby's health, along with some other essential vitamins and minerals.

Babies and children under five can risk running low on vitamins A, C and D. Formula contains all three vitamins and will keep levels topped up, if baby is having her 500ml a day. Breast-fed babies might need a vitamin D top-up in addition to their regular feed (from 1 month old). Ask your health professional for more information about vitamin drops.

* **Vitamin A:** necessary to help develop healthy vision, healthy skin and for maintaining the immune system to protect against infections and viruses. Particularly useful for cold and flu season, if your little one will be attending nursery and play groups.

Vitamin A can be found in three out of four main food groups – milk and dairy (milk, cheese and yogurt), protein-rich foods (liver, eggs, oily fish) and fruits and vegetables in the form of beta-carotene. Beta-carotene, when consumed, turns into vitamin A. Beta-carotene-rich ingredients include: apricots, cantaloupe melons, carrots, mangoes, peaches, pumpkins, butternut squash and sweet potatoes (orange and yellow fruit and vegetables), spinach and red peppers.

Very small amounts of beta-carotene can also be found in dried basil, dried parsley, dried oregano, ground sage and paprika.

* **Vitamin C:** as with vitamin A, vitamin C is vital for little immune systems to help keep infections at bay. It helps protect cells from damage, is necessary for healthy connective tissue and encourages quick healing of cuts and grazes. In addition, vitamin C helps the body absorb iron from non-meat foods, which is extremely important for babies following a vegetarian diet. Vitamin C can be found in: strawberries, plums, raspberries, blueberries, watermelon, citrus fruits (i.e. oranges), kiwi fruit, mango, papaya, melon, red and green peppers, broccoli,

Brussels sprouts, spinach, cabbage, cauliflower, white potatoes and tomatoes.

* **'Sunshine' Vitamin D:** Unlike other vitamins, most of our vitamin D does not come from food but is produced by our bodies – and we need sunlight on our skin for this to happen. Vitamin D is key to regulating the amount of calcium in the body, which is necessary for keeping teeth and bones healthy. Strong bones are vital for helping your little one learn to walk. Vitamin D is found in only a few food sources – oily fish (salmon, mackerel), eggs, liver, fortified breakfast cereals and fortified infant formula.

See previous page for details on topping up vitamin D. But don't forget you can also top up the whole family's vitamin D by playing and spending time outdoors in the sunshine. Just be safe in the sun! Hats and sunscreen are always a good idea.

* **B Vitamins:** This diverse group of vitamins is necessary for converting food into energy, which your little one will need for crawling, walking and playing, and also helps the formation of healthy red blood cells. B vitamins include thiamin (vitamin B1), riboflavin (vitamin B2), niacin (vitamin B3), pantothenic acid (vitamin B5), pyroxidine (vitamin B6), biotin (vitamin B7), folic acid and cobalamin (vitamin B12). Each food group contains a different range of B vitamins.

Vitamin B12 is necessary for the production of healthy red blood cells (with folic acid), nerve function and prevention of a type of anaemia. It is naturally found in animal products – eggs, fish (sardines, salmon and tuna), red meat (lamb and beef), poultry, milk, yogurt, cheese and other dairy products.

Folic acid partners with vitamin B12 in the formation of healthy red blood cells. On its own it is also important for healthy nerve function for baby. Folic acid can be found in vegetables – broccoli, Brussels sprouts, peas and spinach – and also in protein-rich foods including chickpeas, lentils and kidney beans.

* **Iron:** this essential mineral is required for the function of healthy red blood cells, which carry oxygen around the body.

Similar to a squirrel's stockpile of nuts for the winter, your little one will have provisions of iron to last up to the age of 6 months. From that point onwards, her stocks will slowly begin to dwindle. But don't panic. It only needs topping up while you wean your little one onto solid food. From then on she'll get what she needs if she's eating balanced, nutritious meals. So 6 months is a good time to start introducing iron into your little one's diet.

Protein-rich foods are a wonderful source of iron – eggs, lean cuts of beef and lamb, dark chicken meat (legs and thighs), liver (once a week only), pulses such as lentils, chickpeas and kidney beans, nuts (peanut butter is good!). Dried fruit (apricots, figs and prunes), dark leafy green vegetables (spinach, watercress and kale) and fortified breakfast cereals are other valuable sources.

It's important to get iron into your little one's diet, as a diet lacking in iron can lead to anaemia. Try to include an iron-rich food at least once a day when your baby is enjoying solid food.

* **Calcium:** this mineral is required for building strong teeth and bones, regulating muscle contractions in the body (including heartbeat), and ensures the nerve function works effectively.

Calcium is commonly found in milk and dairy produce – whole milk, cheese, yogurt and fromage frais – but can also be found in other food groups you may not be aware of. Other sources of calcium include: some tofu, green leafy vegetables (broccoli, bok choy, spring greens), okra, some nuts, dried fruit (figs, apricots, raisins), bread and some tinned fish (sardines, pilchards or salmon). However, calcium provided by the dairy food group is easily absorbed by our bodies, which is why dairy is the most popular source of calcium.

It's important to note that whole milk MUST NOT be introduced into a baby's diet as a main drink prior to the age of one (for further details see page 181).

* **Zinc:** protein-rich foods are excellent sources of B vitamins and many contain zinc. Zinc, a mineral required for processing proteins, fat and carbs, is also necessary for supporting a good

sense of taste and smell and for healing cuts and wounds efficiently. Exactly what your little one will need when she starts running around causing mischief!

Zinc can be found in poultry, red meat, wholegrain foods and dairy foods such as cheese.

All of these vitamins and minerals,and many more, make an appearance across a range of recipes within this book. And the recipes and meal plans, here, have been developed to assist you in achieving the right balance as your little one grows.

But don't feel you have to stick to my recipes rigidly and do use them in conjunction with other recipes within your chosen weaning plan, if you wish.

You may need to increase or reduce the amount of food you offer, depending on your baby's appetite and needs, so flexibility is essential.

INGREDIENTS YOUR BABY DOESN'T NEED

Before your little one's exciting flavour-led weaning adventure begins, there are a number of foods you should be aware of that will need to be avoided or introduced later as a precaution. And peanuts are not on the list!

Recent research suggests that introducing peanut products into a baby's diet (after 6 months) may reduce the risk of an allergy developing in future. So it's actually a good idea to put some smooth peanut butter and other nut butters on the menu. But do be cautious: discuss the introduction of nuts into your baby's diet with your GP or health visitor. If there's a history of allergies, asthma, eczema, hayfever in your family, you may need to wait until later to be safe.

* **Added Salt** Salt and high-salt foods (like stock-cube) should be avoided as it can damage a baby's immature kidneys. Babies under 1 year old need less than 1g of salt per day, which they usually get from breast milk or formula.

* **Added Sugar** Babies are sweet enough! They don't require any more sugar. Sugar can damage a baby's growing teeth (even before the teeth have emerged) and lead to unnecessary and unhealthy weight gain. This does not apply to natural sugars from fruits, vegetables and in their usual milk.
* **Honey** Occasionally honey contains a bacteria that can cause infant botulism – a rare but very serious illness. So avoid honey until after your baby's first birthday, and even then, use it sparingly – it can contribute to tooth decay.
* **Low-fat Foods** Fat is an important source of concentrated energy for babies and toddlers. Full-fat foods (e.g. milk, yogurt, cheese) are a must for baby until the age of two, after which you can think about introducing low-fat foods if baby is growing well. Beware also of higher sugar levels in low-fat products.
* **Whole Nuts (excludes Nut Butters)** Whole nuts are a choking hazard so shouldn't be offered to your little one until she is at least 5 years old. Peanuts and other nuts can, however, be introduced into a baby's diet in either a crushed or ground form from the age of 6 months. Alternatively you can offer baby peanut butter instead, as long as your little one is not allergic. (Be aware that some contain added salt and sugar.)
* **Runny Eggs** Undercooked eggs may cause food poisoning (salmonella) so no runny yolks for baby just yet. Eggs are safe from 6 months but the whole egg (yolk and white) should be cooked thoroughly (your baby can eat eggs with runny yolks from 1 year). Eggs are also an allergen in some infants so keep an eye on baby when introducing egg for the first time.
* **Shellfish** Undercooked shellfish should never be offered to baby as it can cause food poisoning. Ideally wait until your little one is older (7–9 months old) before introducing it, well cooked, to baby. You will also need to ensure all shellfish is well-cooked.
* **Shark, Swordfish, Marlin** These fish contain high levels of mercury which can affect a baby's developing nervous system, so avoid them. Offer oily fish instead: tuna, salmon or mackerel.

* **Wheat and Gluten** should be avoided prior to the age of 6 months as they can potentially trigger an allergy.

* **Cow's Milk** Avoid cow's milk as a main drink as it lacks the right balance of nutrients for infants under one. Continue with breast milk or formula until your little one's first birthday – the amount will decrease as she fills up on more solid food and you can move to 500–600ml per day. It is then safe to introduce cow's milk as a main drink but it must be whole milk only. Cow's milk is suitable to use in cooking from 6 months.

* **Tea and Coffee** Caffeine not only disrupts a baby's sleep but also reduces iron absorption, which can be detrimental to a baby's health and can potentially increase the risk of anaemia. Offer sips of water with meals instead.

* **Squash, Flavoured Milk and Fizzy Drinks** These drinks aren't necessary for baby. They contain added sugar, which can lead to both tooth decay and weight gain. Offer sips of water with meals instead.

A GOOD DRINK IN ADDITION TO BREAST MILK AND FORMULA

* **Water** If you will be giving your little one water before 6 months, the water must be boiled, then cooled before offering it to your baby.

From 6 months onwards you can offer your little one tap water in addition to her usual milk. Serve water throughout the day with meals and with snacks in either a free-flow beaker or a baby cup.

* **Pure fruit juices**, which state 'not from concentrate' can be offered, occasionally, after baby is 6 months old, but juice must be diluted one part juice to 10 parts water, and served alongside meals to reduce the risk of tooth decay.

GETTING STARTED

Here are some practical bits to be aware of before you begin weaning.

GERM-FREE AND SAFE

When babies are just a few months old, their immune system is still developing so they can be sensitive to germs and viruses. You'll already be aware of this if you formula-feed your little one and currently sterilize your baby's bottle-feeding equipment. If you begin weaning before 6 months, you will need to sterilize the weaning bowls and spoon as well. If you begin weaning from 6 months, this is not necessary.

In either case you do need to adhere to some basic food hygiene rules:

PREPARATION

* Wash your hands
* Wash chopping boards thoroughly and avoid cross-contamination by using separate chopping boards for raw meat and vegetables
* Wash and peel fruit before serving
* Wash baby bowls in hot soapy water and dry them thoroughly (If your little one is younger than 6 months, you will need to sterilize your weaning bowls and spoons)
* Keep pets away! If your pets are anything like my cats, they'll want to cuddle up next to your little one. As cute as this may be, you don't want your pets near food-preparation surfaces.

COOKING/HEATING

* Thoroughly cooked food is a must before serving to baby
* Try to cool food as quickly as possible (it should take no longer than 2 hours), then store as necessary in the refrigerator or freezer.

* Thaw frozen portions overnight in the fridge. Warm food either in a saucepan or in the microwave until piping hot. Allow to cool before serving to baby.
* Never reheat your little one's cooked food or frozen food more than once. Any leftover meals should be discarded.
* Check for hotspots if you warm your little one's food in the microwave. Baby's food should be stirred thoroughly and the temperature must ALWAYS be tested before serving.

FREEZING BABY FOOD

All the freezer friendly recipes in this book are marked with ❄ symbol. When freezing baby food in the early stages, it's best to freeze them in flexible ice-cube trays. Before you place the puree-filled ice-cube trays in the freezer, ensure the tray is covered with a lid or placed inside a freezer bag. It must also be clearly labelled with the contents. Once frozen, pop the baby food cubes out of the tray, place them in a freezer bag, seal, label and date the bag, then pop them back in the freezer.

As your baby grows and her portion size gets larger, you can either defrost 2–3 ice-cubes to make one meal, or you can freeze larger individual portions in good-quality freezer bags, labelling them with the contents and date before you freeze them.

STEAMING

There are different ways to steam fruits and vegetables and they don't require your buying a steamer. I steam my vegetables in the microwave. Here are two easy methods you can try simply using your existing kitchen items.

Microwave Place your vegetables in a microwavable dish, add 2–3 tablespoons of water, cover the dish with either a lid (leaving a small vent) or cling film (piercing a few holes), and steam on high in the microwave until the vegetables are tender.

Homemade Steamer Fill the bottom of a saucepan with a little water, pop vegetables in a colander and into the saucepan and cover with a lid. The steam will rise from the water underneath.

FOOD ESSENTIALS AND KITCHEN TOOLS

You'll need to invest in some essentials for the kitchen. I have split these into food essentials and useful weaning tools. You'll most likely have some of the food essentials already, and you may not need every item straight away, either. Your stock of food essentials will expand the more you cook for your little one.

FOOD ESSENTIALS – CUPBOARD, FRIDGE, FREEZER

Carb-rich (starches)

* Pasta
* Basmati rice
* Potatoes
* Couscous
* Noodles
* Pitta bread
* Rolled/Porridge oats

Fruits and Vegetables

* Tinned plum or chopped tomatoes
* Onions
* Tomato puree
* Dried fruit – raisins, apricots and dates
* Frozen vegetables – peas, sweetcorn, broccoli
* Garlic and ginger – fresh, frozen or bottled

Milk and Dairy

* Full-fat Greek yogurt
* Whole milk
* Cheddar cheese
* Unsalted butter

Protein-rich
* Tinned fish – tuna, salmon, sardines*
* Tinned beans and pulses – kidney beans, butter beans, chickpeas *
* Lentils
* Eggs

Other
* Coconut milk
* Plain flour
* Atta/chapatti flour
* Olive oil

Useful Weaning Tools
* Shallow, soft-tipped weaning spoons
* Weaning bowls
* Bibs and/or long-sleeved bibs
* Food processor/ handheld blender
* Masher
* High chair (with tray)
* Steamer (optional) – see page 31 for alternative ways to steam
* Steriliser (optional) – only required if weaning before 6 months
* Plastic floor mats, or towels (for the floor)
* Ice-cube trays
* Sturdy freezer bags
* Free-flow beaker or baby cup
* Muslin cloths
* Permanent marker pen for labelling bags

*Watch out for added salt or sugar in processed foods, particularly tinned foods.

STAGE 1: PUREES

(AROUND 6 MONTHS/
AT LEAST 17 WEEKS)

You've spotted the ready-for-weaning signs! Your little one is now ready to begin her exciting flavour-led weaning adventure. So, starting from the very root of my flavour-led weaning flower, your little one's palate is preparing to grow by embarking on the basic stage of weaning – first tastes and spoon feeding.

The very first stage of weaning may seem daunting at first, but don't worry, you'll find that it will whizz by very quickly and, before you know it, your baby is ready to move on to stage 2.

THREE-PHASE PROCESS

This chapter is split into three phases. Phase 1 concentrates on simple, single ingredient purees made with everyday fruit and vegetables, to offer within the first two weeks of weaning. After two weeks, or when first tastes have been accepted, move onto phase 2 and mixed ingredient purees (fruit and veg combinations).

After at least a week of phase 2, and from 6 months, phase 3 can take place. When your baby is happily slurping up mixed ingredient purees she is ready for the 'flavour switch' – mixed ingredient purees with single herbs and spices added.

READY FOR STAGE 1 (PHASE 1) FLAVOUR-LED WEANING CHECKLIST:

☐ Baby is around 6 months of age and at least 17 weeks old

☐ Baby is able to sit up straight

☐ Baby is holding head steady

☐ Baby grabs for a spoon and makes co-ordinated movements

☐ Baby's tongue-thrust reflex has disappeared and she can swallow food

IDEAL TIME OF DAY

Lunchtime is often the best time of day for introducing new flavours (although this might vary depending on your baby's routine), as your little one should be sufficiently hungry, but not too tired to eat.

A SPOONFUL OR TWO

Flavour-led weaning is about exposing your baby's palate to lots of different tastes at the very beginning, and less about the amount that goes in. So one or two weaning spoonfuls of puree just before, or just after, a milk feed will be enough. I suggest starting off with one puree a day and then progress to two a day, if it suits your baby (see page 51).

TEXTURE

At this stage baby is only used to drinking milk so any texture much thicker than this will most likely be a struggle (definitely from 4 months, less so from 6). Purees should be smooth, no thinner than your baby's usual milk otherwise it won't stay on the spoon, and no thicker than runny honey. Achieve super-smooth purees by passing them through a sieve before serving, although this isn't necessary for all purees. Remember to feed baby with soft-tipped weaning spoons.

MILK FEEDS

At this stage your little one is still very small, so milk feeds – her 'complete food' – will be an integral part of her diet and the source of most of her nutrients. So continue with her regular milk feeds (breast milk or formula) as normal to ensure baby is consuming all of the nutrients necessary for healthy growth.

KEEPING THE NUTRIENTS

As I have mentioned, preserving the nutrients in fruit and vegetables is vital for baby. Whether you steam, boil or bake your fruits and vegetables, the key to ensuring nutrients are preserved is to avoid overcooking them.

If you choose to boil vegetables, keep the boiled water. This extra liquid may come in handy for thinning out your little one's purees and it will also contain nutrients that were released from the vegetables when they were cooking. If your preference is to steam fruit and vegetables, see page 31 for details.

ALLERGIES

It's always a good idea to be cautious when introducing any new foods into your little one's diet (see page 19). The first taste recipes in this book are low-allergen foods so are unlikely to cause an allergic reaction. It doesn't hurt, however, to be mindful of allergic reaction symptoms, just to be on the safe side.

Keep an eye out for tummy upsets, skin rashes, swelling of the lips and face, shortness of breath, runny and blocked noses, sneezing, itchy watery eyes, nausea, vomiting and diarrhoea. Cow's milk and other dairy, eggs, fish, nuts (including peanuts, cashews, almonds, hazelnuts, pistachios and nut products), seeds, soya products (including tofu), shellfish and foods containing wheat or gluten should not be introduced before 6 months.

FIRST TASTE FACE!

Don't be surprised if your little one looks a little shell-shocked, as though she is going to vomit, or scrunches up her face from the first taste. Aaliyah did all three! Then she tilted her head to one side, lip-smacking away in deep thought. If I could have attached a speech bubble to her head it would have read 'Hmmm…. This is new! Not sure I trust it… oh no, wait a minute – I think I do!' Shortly after she leaned forward and opened her mouth for the second spoonful.

DON'T FORGET ABOUT FLAVOURS

While introducing new flavours is important to keep variety in your little one's diet, don't forget about the old ones! Continue to offer accepted tastes alongside new tastes, so baby doesn't forget about them.

FREEZING PUREES

Nearly all of the purees in this book can be made ahead (in about 5–10 minutes) and frozen. (Look for the freezer symbol ❄.) If you plan to freeze your baby's purees, thin them after you defrost them with formula or breast milk.

PHASE 1:
FIRST 2 WEEKS
SINGLE INGREDIENT PUREES

There's very little need to develop a baby's sweet taste buds, as babies are born with a natural sweet tooth and a mother's milk is naturally sweet. I recommend, from experience, beginning with sweet root vegetables – carrots, parsnips and sweet potato. Why? Root vegetables are nutrient-dense and your baby will already be accustomed to having yummy sweet milk in her mouth. So, offering sweet first tastes will encourage her to accept solid food initially. Then you can start introducing mild savoury flavours.

All the purees in this book take about 5–10 minutes to make.

MAKES
16 ICE-CUBES

MAKES
12 ICE-CUBES

SWEET POTATO PUREE ❄

Wash and scrub 1 medium sweet potato. Prick it all over with a fork and pop it in the microwave to cook on high for 6–7 minutes, or until tender to the touch. Alternatively, bake it in a preheated oven at 200°C/400°F/gas mark 6 for up to 45 minutes, or until tender.

Once cooled cut the potato in half lengthways, scoop out the flesh and place it in a food processor (or use a handheld blender). Add at least 3–4 tablespoons of cooled boiled water or your baby's usual milk to thin out the puree, as sweet potato has a thicker consistency than other vegetables. Blend until smooth and add extra water or milk as necessary to achieve the perfect texture for your little one.

PARSNIP OR CARROT PUREE ❄

Peel and trim both ends of 2 medium parsnips or carrots. If you're making parsnip puree, cut them in half lengthways and cut out the hard woody core before continuing.

Roughly chop the parsnip or carrot and steam for 3½ minutes until tender. Alternatively, transfer to a saucepan with 4 tablespoons of water and simmer (covered) on low heat until tender.

Pop the parsnip or carrot into a food processor (or use a handheld blender), add 1–2 tablespoons of cooled boiled water or your baby's usual milk, and blend until smooth.

SWEET PEA PUREE ❄

Steam 100g of frozen peas for 2–2½ minutes until tender and vibrant green in colour. Alternatively, place the peas in a saucepan with 2 tablespoons of water and simmer (covered) on low heat for 2–2½ minutes until tender.

Pop into a food processor (or use a handheld blender), add 2 tablespoons of cooled boiled water or your baby's usual milk, and blend until super smooth. Add extra water or milk if required to achieve the perfect consistency for your little one.

CREAMY CAULIFLOWER PUREE ❄

Steam 100g (about ¼ head) of cauliflower (thoroughly washed, cut into small florets) for 5–6 minutes until tender. Alternatively, place in a saucepan with 4 tablespoons of water and simmer (covered) on low heat until tender.

Pop the florets into a food processor (or use a handheld blender), add 2 tablespoons of cooled boiled water or your baby's usual milk, and blend until smooth. Add extra water or milk as necessary.

BROCCOLI PUREE ❄

Steam 100g (about ½ head) of broccoli (thoroughly washed, cut into small florets) for 3½–4 minutes until tender. Alternatively, place in a saucepan with 3–4 tablespoons of water and simmer (covered) on low heat until tender.

Pop the broccoli into a food processor (or use a handheld blender), add 2 tablespoons of cooled boiled water or your baby's usual milk, and blend until smooth. Add extra water or milk as necessary, then pass the puree through a sieve (to remove any lingering fibres).

WHITE POTATO PUREE ❄

Wash, peel and cube 1 medium potato (about 250g) and place the cubes in a saucepan. Cover with water, bring to the boil and cook for 8–10 minutes until tender. Alternatively, steam the cubes for up to 20 minutes (checking halfway through the cooking time) until tender.

Drain the potato and place in a bowl with 6 tablespoons of cooled boiled water or your baby's usual milk. Mash using a masher or fork until smooth, adding extra milk or water as necessary to achieve the perfect consistency for your baby.

AUBERGINE PUREE ❄

Wash and peel 1 medium, shiny aubergine (about 250g). Cut the flesh into chunks and steam for 8–10 minutes, or until tender.

Pop the flesh into a food processor (or use a handheld blender) along with 2 tablespoons of cooled boiled water or your baby's usual milk, and blend until smooth. Add more liquid as necessary.

Pass the puree through a sieve to ensure the little seeds are removed before serving to your little one. For older babies you can mash the aubergine instead of pureeing it, for a rougher texture. The little steamed pieces make a great finger food for babies, too.

AVOCADO PUREE (NO-COOK)

Cut a ripe avocado in half, remove and discard the stone and scoop out the flesh. Pop the flesh into a food processor along with 2 tablespoons of cooled boiled water or your baby's usual milk (more for a thinner consistency) and blend until smooth. (This could also be mashed for older babies.) Serve immediately.

BANANA PUREE (NO-COOK)

Peel and chop a ripe banana. Place it in a bowl and mash with the back of a fork. Add some of your baby's usual milk and mash it further to achieve the perfect smooth consistency for your little one.

APPLE OR PEAR PUREE ❄

Wash, peel, core and chop 2 sweet apples (Gala or Pink Lady are good) or 2 pears. Steam for 2½–3 minutes until tender. Alternatively, place in a saucepan with 2–3 tablespoons of water and simmer (covered) on low heat until the fruit is tender. Pop the cooked apple or pear in a food processor (or use a handheld blender) and blend until super smooth. Add a little cooled boiled water or your baby's usual milk to thin out the puree as necessary.

TIP ~

If the pear is ripe and soft, there is no need to steam it beforehand. Simply peel, core, chop and mash until smooth.

MANGO PUREE ❄
(NO-COOK)

Wash the skin of 1 very ripe mango thoroughly. Stand the mango upright on a flat surface and slice down the thickest part of the mango, avoiding the stone.

Using this slice, make horizontal and vertical cuts in the flesh to create a cross-hatch of cubes and push the bottom of the skin to create a 'hedgehog'. Repeat for the other half.

Cut off the cubes, pop them into a food processor (or use a handheld blender) and blend until smooth. Add a little cooled boiled water or some of your baby's usual milk to loosen the puree as necessary.

As baby grows, mash the mango cubes instead of pureeing, for extra texture.

PAPAYA PUREE ❄
(NO-COOK)

Wash 1 papaya, cut it in half lengthways and scoop out the seeds. Either remove the skin, or scoop out the flesh from both halves, and chop. Papaya flesh naturally contains a lot of water, so don't add any extra liquid to thin out the puree.

Pop the flesh into a food processor (or use a handheld blender) and blend until smooth, or mash the flesh. Pass the puree through a sieve to remove any stringy fibres before serving.

As baby grows, mash the papaya flesh instead of pureeing for extra texture.

APRICOT OR PLUM PUREE ❄
(NO-COOK)

Wash 2 ripe apricots (or plums), cut them in half and twist to pull apart. Peel the skin using a sharp knife and remove the stones. Roughly chop the flesh, pop it into a food processor and blend until smooth. Alternatively, steam for 1½–2 minutes, or until the flesh is soft, before blending in a food processor (or use a handheld blender). Pass the puree through a sieve and serve.

TIP ~

I found plum and apricot purees were great for relieving constipation, so if your little one has a bout of diarrhoea, I would hold off offering these purees to her until she is feeling better.

MELON PUREE
(NO-COOK)

Cut 4–5 cubes of flesh from a ripe melon (watermelon, honeydew or cantaloupe work well), ensuring the seeds and skin have been cut away. Pop the flesh into a food processor (or use a handheld blender) and blend until smooth, or mash the flesh.

TIP ~

Melon contains a lot of water so there's no need to add extra liquid. This puree is best served straight away.

MEAL PLANS — FOR FIRST TWO WEEKS

Try these suggested combinations in addition to your baby's regular milk feeds.

DAY	LUNCH
MONDAY	Carrot puree
TUESDAY	Sweet potato puree
WEDNESDAY	Cauliflower puree
THURSDAY	Parsnip puree
FRIDAY	Apple puree
SATURDAY	Aubergine puree
SUNDAY	Mango puree

DAY	BREAKFAST	LUNCH
MONDAY	Pear puree	White potato puree
TUESDAY	Papaya puree	Cauliflower puree
WEDNESDAY	Mango puree	Aubergine puree
THURSDAY	Banana puree	Carrot puree
FRIDAY	Pear puree	Sweet potato puree
SATURDAY	Apricot puree	Parsnip puree
SUNDAY	Apple puree	Avocado puree

PHASE 2:
MIXED INGREDIENT PUREES

After two weeks, or when first tastes have been accepted, move onto mixed ingredient purees, combining simple flavours to create new ones. You can also make your own mixed ingredient purees by combining cubes of frozen purees you have sitting in the freezer, to create your own brand-new flavours for baby.

If weaning from 6 months, you only need to offer mixed ingredient purees for about a week before moving onto phase 3 (page 61). If, however, you are weaning your little one from 4 or 5 months, stay on phase 2 (mixed ingredient purees) for longer, until she is 6 months old.

All the recipes in this section take no more than 10 minutes to make.

BANANA AND AVOCADO PUREE
(NO-COOK)

½ ripe banana – peeled, roughly chopped
½ ripe avocado – stone removed

Place the banana pieces in a bowl and scoop out the avocado flesh. Roughly chop the avocado and pop it into the bowl with the banana. Add 2 tablespoons of your baby's usual milk and mash together with a fork. Alternatively place in a food processor (or use a handheld blender) and blend until smooth. Serve to baby straight away.

PAPAYA, MANGO AND ORANGE PUREE
(NO-COOK)

½ papaya – seeds and skin removed, roughly chopped
½ mango – skin removed, roughly chopped
1 tsp freshly squeezed orange juice

Place the papaya, mango and orange juice in a food processor (or use a handheld blender) and blend until smooth. Add cooled boiled water if necessary to further thin out the puree.

AUBERGINE & CAULIFLOWER PUREE ❄

120g aubergine – washed,
peeled, cubed
100g cauliflower florets
– washed, chopped

Steam the aubergine and cauliflower for 5–6 minutes or until tender. Pop the tender veggies into a food processor (or use a handheld blender), along with 2 tablespoons of cooled boiled water or your baby's usual milk, and blend until smooth. Pass the puree through a sieve to ensure the little aubergine seeds are removed before serving to your little one.

STRAWBERRY, RASPBERRY & BLUEBERRY PUREE (NO-COOK)

70g strawberries –
washed, hulled
30g raspberries – washed
55g blueberries – washed

Pop the strawberries, raspberries and blueberries into a food processor (or use a handheld blender) and blend until smooth. Pass the puree through a sieve to remove the seeds, and serve to baby.

PEA & PEAR PUREE ❄

2 pears – washed, peeled,
 cored, chopped
60g frozen peas

~ TIP ~

If the pear is ripe and
soft, there is no need
to steam it beforehand.
Simply mash until smooth
before combining with
the cooked peas.

Steam the pears for 2½–3 minutes until tender, and the
peas for 2–2½ minutes until tender. Alternatively, put
the pears and peas in a saucepan with 2–3 tablespoons
of water and simmer (covered) until tender. Pop the
peas and pears into a food processor (or use a handheld
blender) and blend until smooth. Add cooled boiled
water or your baby's usual milk to thin out the puree
as necessary.

A WEEK'S MEAL PLAN – FOR PHASE 2

DAY	BREAKFAST	LUNCH
MONDAY	Mango puree with porridge**	Banana and avocado puree
TUESDAY	Apricot puree with full-fat Greek yogurt**	Aubergine and cauliflower puree with rice
WEDNESDAY	Pea and pear puree	Sweet potato puree
THURSDAY	Papaya, mango and orange puree	Carrot and parsnip* puree with rice
FRIDAY	Avocado puree with scrambled eggs**	Strawberry, raspberry and blueberry puree
SATURDAY	Papaya puree with full-fat Greek yogurt**	Sweet potato and broccoli*
SUNDAY	Apple puree with porridge**	Apricot and plum*

* Create these purees by combining remaining ice-cubes from the first two weeks to save time and avoid wastage.

** Eggs, yogurt, porridge and oats are not suitable until 6 months. If your baby is younger, offer her the fruit or vegetable purees on their own. Eggs must be well cooked.

PORRIDGE & RICE

As your little one begins to eat more solids, from 6 months you can introduce porridge, as mentioned in my Week 3 Meal Plan (page 57), along with purees to make more filling meals. Rice can be given before 6 months because it doesn't contain gluten.

MAKES
2–3
SERVINGS

SIMPLE PORRIDGE

150ml whole milk
20g porridge oats

Porridge is a source of fibre and, being carb-rich, it is great for energy, so makes an excellent start to the day for baby.

Place the milk and oats in a saucepan and bring to the boil gently on low heat. Simmer for 4–5 minutes until tender, then pop it into a food processor and blend until smooth. Add your baby's usual milk or cooled boiled water to thin out the porridge as necessary. Remove a small serving (1–2 teaspoons) and swirl into a fruit puree of your choice. Serve to baby warm.

Any remaining porridge can be placed in a container once cool, and stored in the fridge for a day. Reheat in a saucepan or in the microwave, adding some cooled boiled water or some of your baby's usual milk to loosen it. Check for hotspots before serving.

SIMPLE RICE

25g white basmati rice
– washed, drained
90ml water

Baby rice can be bought from the supermarket and mixed with your little one's purees for a more substantial meal. I wouldn't recommend using it very often, however, as it is a processed food. Instead, use homemade mushy basmati rice – it's so simple to cook.

Place the rice in a saucepan, pour in the water, stir and bring to the boil. Simmer (covered) on low heat for 10–12 minutes until the water has been absorbed and the rice is tender and a little mushy. Cool the rice then pop it in a food processor (or use a handheld blender) and blend until smooth, adding more water if necessary. Thin out the rice with cooled boiled water or your baby's usual milk. Remove a small serving (1–2 teaspoons) and swirl into a vegetable puree of your choice. Serve to baby warm.

Any leftover rice should be cooled quickly, then can be placed in a container and stored in the fridge for a day. Reheat it in the microwave, checking for hotspots before serving (it should only be reheated once).

PHASE 3:
THE FLAVOUR
SWITCH
(BETWEEN 6 AND 7 MONTHS)

If your little one has accepted first tastes and is happily slurping up basic mixed ingredient purees, and she is at least 6 months old, then it's time to progress to mixed ingredient purees with a little zing (single herb or spice additions).

These 'zingy' extra ingredients in these purees, although used here in small amounts, are all reputed to offer health benefits for your little one's diet. Garlic, turmeric and cardamom are natural immune-system boosters, while I've had success with relieving teething pains with a little yummy sweet cinnamon or warming nutmeg (try my Chewable Teething Sticks on page 136, Gum Soothing Squash on page 107 or Beetroot, apple and clove puree on page 76). See pages 215–16 for my homemade remedies to help a restless baby sleep, prevent colds and flu, help soothe a gassy baby and more.

SIGNS THAT YOUR BABY IS READY FOR PHASE 3 FLAVOUR-LED WEANING:

☐ First tastes accepted

☐ Simple mixed ingredient purees (fruit and vegetable combinations) accepted

☐ Happily slurping two meals a day (most likely breakfast and lunch)

STARTED WEANING AT 6 MONTHS?

If, like me, you're a stickler for the weaning at 6 months rule, don't start your little one's weaning journey at phase 3. It's important you start at the very beginning of phase 1 on page 36 – first tastes. After two weeks you can continue onto mixed ingredient purees, or skip it and head straight onto the 'flavour-switch feeding plan' on page 65 and continue from that point.

TWO MEALS A DAY

Continue feeding your little one two meals a day, so she can enjoy eating different flavours in the same day. This could be breakfast and lunch, or lunch and an afternoon snack.

TEXTURE

Purees should still be fairly smooth but you can think about making them a little more substantial. Chewing is excellent for developing motor skills and developing tongue muscles to help with speech. So the sooner you can move on from super-smooth purees the better. Make purees thicker or more textured by using less liquid, combining with rice or pureeing them less.

SOLID FOOD AND MILK FEEDS

At this stage your little one will begin to consume more food (1–2 ice-cubes) per meal in contrast to the couple of spoonfuls of solids you initially started with.

She will still need 500–600ml of breast milk or formula per day to continue providing her with valuable nutrients. At this stage she won't be eating a wide enough range of solids, so it's important you continue with the milk feeds.

VITAMINS

Vitamins A, C and D are key vitamins babies needs to consume for healthy growth and development. Speak with your doctor or health visitor for more details on supplements, and see page 23 for some additional key vitamins and minerals required for healthy growth.

ALLERGENS

The following foods are safe to introduce now that your little one is 6 months old, however there is a chance allergic reactions could be triggered, so introduce each food one at a time, in small amounts, while keeping an eye out for allergic reaction (see page 19).

* Cow's milk (in meals only) and other dairy
* Eggs – make sure you cook them thoroughly (white and yolk)
* Fish – all bones should be removed
* Ground nuts, peanut butter and peanut products
* Seeds
* Shellfish (fully cooked, see page 28)
* Wheat (and other grains containing gluten)
* Soy products

GROWTH SPURT ALERT!

You might feel your baby experiences a growth spurt at around 6 months. She may seem hungrier than normal, drinking more milk, more frequently. She may also sleep for longer, or sleep less (in my case!).

Now onto my flavour-switch feeding plan....

FLAVOUR-SWITCH FEEDING PLAN

This is a very simple one-week feeding plan to help transition your little one safely from basic tastes to basic tastes with herbs and spices. Why? Well it's prudent to make sure your little one doesn't have an allergic reaction to spices. While an allergic reaction is very unlikely, it may occur. So this plan allows you to introduce one spice, one day at a time so you can keep an eye out for allergic reactions, and identify the little culprit that may cause them!

As baby will now be consuming two meals a day, one of the meals you offer should be a puree from this flavour-switch feeding plan.

I've given timings in this chapter for all the recipes that take more than 15 minutes to make. Everything else can be made in under 15 minutes.

DAY	BREAKFAST	LUNCH
MONDAY	Banana puree with porridge	Apple and ginger puree
TUESDAY	Apple and pear puree* with full-fat Greek yogurt	Pea and mint puree
WEDNESDAY	Pea and pear puree with mushy rice	Banana and cinnamon puree
THURSDAY	Strawberry, raspberry and blueberry puree	Pear and cardamom puree
FRIDAY	Mango and apple puree* with full-fat Greek yogurt	Plum and vanilla puree
SATURDAY	Pear and banana puree* with full-fat Greek yogurt	Butternut squash and cumin puree
SUNDAY	Papaya, mango and orange puree with porridge	Cauliflower and turmeric puree

*Create these purees by combining remaining ice-cubes from the first two weeks to save time and avoid wastage, or – if you have no leftover cubes of puree – see pages 40–49 (Stage 1 puree recipes).

APPLE & GINGER PUREE ❄

2 sweet Gala apples
(or any other sweet
variety) – washed,
peeled, cored, cubed
¼ tsp minced ginger

Yummy, sweet puree with a hint of ginger for baby.
I think this is great for combating coughs and settling
nausea.

~ TIP ~

Swap the ginger for a
large pinch of ground
cinnamon for a yummy
apple and cinnamon puree.

Place the apples, 4 tablespoons of water and ginger in
a saucepan and stir. Simmer (covered) on low heat for
6–8 minutes until the apples are tender. Pop into a food
processor (or use a handheld blender) and blend until
super smooth, adding extra cooled boiled water to thin
the puree if necessary.

PEA & MINT PUREE ❄

120g frozen peas
2 small mint leaves,
    washed

A beautiful spring-green puree. Peas are a valuable
source of vitamin C and several B vitamins for your baby.

Steam the peas for 2–2½ minutes until tender.
Alternatively, place the peas in a saucepan with
2 tablespoons of water and simmer (covered) on low
heat for 2–2½ minutes until tender. Pop them into a
food processor (or use a handheld blender) along with
the mint leaves and blend until smooth. Add extra
cooled boiled water to thin the puree if necessary.

BANANA & CINNAMON PUREE (NO-COOK)

½ ripe banana – peeled,
    roughly chopped
Pinch of ground
    cinnamon

This is so sweet and fragrant. Bananas are high in potassium which is vital to heart function and rich in carbohydrate to fuel your baby's exploration of her world.

Place the banana in a bowl with the ground cinnamon and 2 tablespoons of your baby's usual milk, or cooled boiled water. Mash together using a fork to achieve the perfect consistency for baby, adding more liquid if necessary. Alternatively, blend until smooth using a handheld blender or in a food processor.

Monday **Tuesday** **Wednesday** **Thursday**

Friday **Saturday** **Sunday**

PEAR & CARDAMOM PUREE ❄

2 pears – peeled, cored, cubed
Pinch of ground cardamom or 1 whole green cardamom pod

This is subtle and mildly sweet. Cardamom is reputed to help settle flatulence and help with teething pain.

Place the pears in a saucepan with 4 tablespoons of water and cardamom. Stir and simmer (covered) on low heat for 5–6 minutes until the pears are tender, then remove the cardamom pod if using a whole one. Pop the cooked pear into a food processor (or use a handheld blender) and blend until smooth, or mash (for a rougher texture).

MAKES
10 ICE-CUBES

PLUM & VANILLA PUREE ❄

2 plums – washed,
    peeled, stone removed,
    roughly chopped
1 vanilla pod

Sweet or a little sour at times, plums are an excellent source of vitamin C and I find they are great for helping a constipated baby. Vanilla is fragrant and sweet.

~~~~~~~

~ TIPS ~

* If the puree is too sour, add a little mashed banana when serving. Alternatively, simmer the plums in 2 tablespoons of pure apple juice.

* The rest of the vanilla pod can be stored in a plastic zip-seal bag with the air squeezed out of it, or in an airtight container. Store in a cool, dry place away from direct sunlight and use within a few weeks.

Place the chopped plums in a saucepan with 2 tablespoons of water. Cut the tip off the vanilla pod, slice it in half lengthwise just halfway down the length of the pod and scrape out the vanilla seeds with the tip of the knife into the pan. Stir and simmer (covered) on low heat for 4–6 minutes, or until the plums are tender. If the plums are already fairly ripe, simmer for just a couple of minutes to combine the vanilla seeds with the flesh. Pop the cooked plum into a food processor (or use a handheld blender) and blend until smooth, or mash (for a rougher texture).

CAULIFLOWER & TURMERIC PUREE ❄

100g (about ¼ head)
cauliflower – washed,
cut into small florets
Pinch of ground turmeric

Cauliflower is rich in antioxidant vitamin C, and turmeric is good for lots of things, including boosting memory and immunity, and settling indigestion.

Place the cauliflower and turmeric in a saucepan along with 5 tablespoons of water and stir. Simmer (covered) on low heat for 5–8 minutes until the cauliflower is tender. Pop the cooked cauliflower into a food processor (or use a handheld blender) along with ½ tablespoon of cooled boiled water and blend until smooth, adding extra water to thin the puree as necessary, or mash (for a rougher texture).

BUTTERNUT SQUASH & CUMIN PUREE ❄

250g butternut squash
(about ½ butternut
squash) – peeled,
deseeded, cubed
Pinch of ground cumin

Butternut squash is a rich source of beta-carotene
(a form of vitamin A), a key vitamin for babies.
Vitamin A is vital for immunity and cumin is reputed
to hold immune-boosting properties too.

Place the butternut squash in a saucepan with
5 tablespoons of water and cumin. Stir and simmer
(covered) on low heat for 10–12 minutes until tender
(checking halfway through the cooking time). Pop the
cooked squash into a food processor (or use a handheld
blender) and blend until smooth, adding extra cooled
boiled water to the thin the puree as necessary, or
mash (for a rougher texture).

MIXED INGREDIENT PUREES WITH SINGLE FLAVOUR ADDITIONS (BETWEEN 6 AND 7 MONTHS)

Flavour-switch feeding plan complete, now baby is ready for mixed ingredient purees with single flavour additions – the zing!

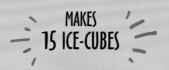

MAKES
15 ICE-CUBES

TOTAL PREP &
COOKING TIME:
15 MINS

VANILLA RICE WITH MANGO PUREE ❄

50g white basmati rice
 – washed, drained
180ml water
1 vanilla pod – split
 lengthways
130g mango (about
 1 small ripe mango) –
 washed, flesh cubed
 (see page 47 for
 'hedgehog' technique)

This breakfast dish or pudding is creamy, sweet and fragrant. Mangoes are rich in beta-carotene (a form of vitamin A) – excellent for eye health, asthma prevention and immune-system function. They are also rich in vitamin C and fibre, and include small amounts of iron and calcium.

Place the rice in a saucepan, pour in the water, and add a small pinch of vanilla seeds (scraped from the vanilla pod) and stir. Bring to the boil then simmer (covered) on low heat for 10–12 minutes until the water has been absorbed and the rice is tender and a little mushy. Cool the rice then pop it in a food processor (or use a handheld blender) along with the mango cubes, and blend to a smooth puree. Add cooled boiled water or your baby's usual milk to thin out the puree as necessary.

KIWI, MINT & LIME PUREE ❄️

2 pears – washed, peeled, cored, cubed
½ ripe kiwi
3 mint leaves – washed, chopped
5 drops of fresh lime juice

I LOVE, LOVE, LOVE this one! It's a beautiful puree – fresh, sweet, sour and uplifting. Kiwis and limes are an excellent source of vitamin C, necessary for cold and flu protection. The mint is fresh-tasting and aids digestion. A wonderful combination of flavours.

~ TIPS ~

* If the pears are very ripe, you will not need to cook them to soften them – just pop the cubes straight into the food processor.

* Substitute the pears for apples.

* Develop your little one's sour taste buds by increasing the tang-factor – try 1 pear, 1 kiwi, and the same amount of mint and lime. Sour, but good!

Place the pear cubes in a saucepan with 2 tablespoons of water and simmer (covered) on low heat for 4–5 minutes until tender (alternatively, steam them). Pop them into a food processor.

Next, scoop out the flesh from the half kiwi and pop it into the food processor along with the mint leaves and lime. Blend until smooth, then pass the puree through a sieve to remove the little kiwi pips before serving to baby.

BEETROOT, APPLE & CLOVE PUREE ❄

100g beetroot (about
  1 beetroot) – scrubbed,
  washed, peeled, sliced
1 sweet eating apple –
  peeled, cored, cubed
4 whole cloves

This super-yummy, sweet, brightly coloured puree is high in antioxidants. Beetroot is a good source of iron and folic acid and the fibre can encourage baby's bowel movement – great for constipated babies. Cloves can help to ease teething pain and are anti-fungal.

Steam the beetroot for 5–6 minutes until tender. While the beetroot is cooking, take 4 apple cubes and pierce each piece with a single clove, flower bud end up. Place all of the apple cubes, including the ones studded with cloves, in a saucepan with 3 tablespoons of water and simmer (covered) on low heat until tender. Remove from the heat and remove and discard the whole cloves. Pop the clove-infused apple and tender beetroot into a food processor (or use a handheld blender) and blend until smooth. Use cooled boiled water to thin out the puree as necessary.

CALMING CUCUMBER PUREE (NO-COOK)

5cm length of cucumber
– washed, peeled,
deseeded
2 fresh mint leaves –
washed, chopped
½ tsp full-fat Greek
yogurt

I've found this puree to be great for calming indigestion and relieving trapped wind. Cucumber and cooling mint helps to settle a little stomach. Avoid lentils, beans and cruciferous vegetables if your baby is suffering from trapped wind.

~~~~~~

Place all of the ingredients into a food processor (or use a handheld blender) and blend until super smooth. Pass the puree through a sieve, if necessary, before serving to baby.

MAKES
22 ICE-CUBES

TOTAL PREP & COOKING TIME:
15 MINS

SWEET POTATO, COCONUT & LIME PUREE ❄

225g sweet potato (about 1 sweet potato) – washed, peeled, cubed
150ml water
75ml unsweetened coconut milk (organic)
2 drops of fresh lime juice
3 coriander leaves – fresh, washed

This combines two contrasting flavours for baby – sweet and sour. Yummy sweet potato is rich in beta-carotene which converts into vitamin A in the body (excellent for healthy eyes, skin and immune system). The sour taste (with a hint of sweet) comes from the lime juice .

Place the sweet potato in a saucepan along with the water and coconut milk. Gently bring to the boil on low heat, then simmer (uncovered) for 10–12 minutes until the potato is tender. Pop the sweet potato in a food processor (or use a handheld blender), add the lime juice, 1 tablespoon of the coconut milk the potato was poached in, and throw in the coriander leaves. Blend until smooth. Add cooled boiled water or your baby's usual milk to thin out the puree as necessary.

MANGO & KIWI COLD PREVENTION (NO-COOK)

½ ripe mango
½ ripe kiwi
Pinch of ground
   cinnamon

Mango, rich in beta-carotene (pre-vitamin A), helps to maintain immunity. Combined with vitamin C from the kiwi, this can assist your child in fighting colds and flu.

Place the mango, kiwi and cinnamon into a food processor (or use a handheld blender) and blend until smooth. Pass the puree through a sieve to ensure all the kiwi seeds are removed before serving to baby.

MAKES
22 ICE-CUBES

CREAMY TROPICAL FRUIT PUREE (NO-COOK)

½ ripe banana –
   peeled, chopped
5 blueberries – washed
¼ papaya – peeled,
   deseeded, cubed
1 tbsp plain unsweetened
   yogurt
Pinch of ground ginger

Between them, bananas, blueberries and papaya are sources of potassium, vitamin K and beta-carotene – necessary for all-round good health. Ginger supports healthy digestion and immune system.

Place the banana, blueberries, papaya, yogurt and ginger into a food processor (or use a handheld blender) and blend until smooth. Pass the puree through a sieve to remove fibres and the blueberry skins for a super-smooth puree. For older babies mash rather than blend for extra texture.

STRAWBERRY, BASIL & BANANA PUREE (NO-COOK)

2 strawberries – washed,
    hulled, quartered
½ basil leaf – fresh,
    washed, patted dry
½ ripe banana – peeled,
    chopped

Yummy! Basil is sweet with a hint of bitterness – a new flavour for baby. This makes a delicious, healthy smoothie for adults, too.

Pop the strawberries, basil leaf and banana into a food processor (or use a handheld blender) and blend until smooth. Pass through a sieve and serve. Add cooled boiled water or your baby's usual milk as necessary.

AVOCADO, PAPAYA & CINNAMON PUREE

½ ripe avocado –
   stone removed
½ papaya – peeled,
   deseeded, cubed
Pinch of ground
   cinnamon
3 drops of fresh lemon
   juice

Avocados are creamy, mild-tasting and nutrient-dense. Papaya, like mangoes, are sweet and rich in beta-carotene (a form of vitamin A), great for healthy eyes and skin. Cinnamon supports a healthy immune system and can help to boost memory.

Scoop out the flesh of the avocado and pop it into a food processor (or use a handheld blender), along with the papaya and cinnamon and lemon juice. Blend until smooth and add cooled boiled water or your baby's usual milk to thin out the puree as necessary.

SWEDE, CHEESE & CHIVE PUREE ❄

200g swede (about ½) –
  peeled, cubed
100ml water
60g cauliflower – washed,
  cut into small florets
15g medium Cheddar
  cheese – grated
½ tsp dried chives

Swede is mild and savoury in taste. A great first food for baby, it is rich in vitamin C. Chives are deliciously oniony in taste and nutrient-dense.

Place the swede in a saucepan with the water and simmer (covered) on low heat for 20–25 minutes until tender. While the swede is cooking, steam the cauliflower for 3–4 minutes until tender. Add the cauliflower to a food processor (or use a handheld blender) along with the tender swede, 1 tablespoon of the swede cooking water, the grated cheese and chives, and blend until smooth. Add extra cooled boiled water or your baby's usual milk to thin out the puree as necessary.

SAAG ALOO PUREE ❄

1 tbsp olive oil
100g white potato (about 1 medium white potato) – washed, peeled, cubed
½ tsp minced garlic
40g spinach leaves – washed, stems removed, roughly chopped

~ TIP ~

You can pop the spinach and steamed garlicky potato into a food processor and blend if you wish, however the texture may be a little gloopy or sticky for your little one. Mashed potato has a more palatable texture.

Leafy green spinach has good levels of iron, but even higher levels of vitamins A, K, and folic acid bring a host of health benefits. Garlic is anti-viral.

Heat the oil in a saucepan, add the potato and garlic and sauté for 30 seconds to 1 minute on low heat, then add 5 tablespoons of water and cover. Allow the potato to steam gently for 10 minutes, or until tender.

While the potato is cooking, steam the spinach for 1½–2 minutes until wilted (there is no need to add extra water). Once the spinach is wilted pop it in a food processor (or use a handheld blender) and blend until smooth, then set aside.

Once the garlicky potato is cooked, pop it in a bowl and mash with a masher or fork, adding cooled boiled water or your baby's usual milk to loosen the texture. Keep doing this until you've reached the perfect smooth, runny consistency for baby, then add the pureed spinach and stir to combine well.

SQUASHY DHAL PUREE ❄

30g red lentils – soaked
in water (5–10 mins),
washed, drained
150ml water
¼ tsp ground cumin
200g (about ½) butternut
squash – peeled,
deseeded, cubed

Lentils (dhal) are a good source of iron and protein
for baby – necessary for healthy growth. Beta-carotene
(a form of vitamin A) in subtly sweet squash is great for
the development of healthy vision and skin. Both the
squash and cumin boost immunity.

Place the lentils in a saucepan and add the water, cumin
and squash. Stir, bring to the boil and simmer on low
heat (covered) for 15 minutes or until the lentils and
squash are tender and begin to mush together. Transfer
to a food processor (or use a handheld blender) and
blend until smooth. Add cooled boiled water or your
baby's usual milk to thin out the puree as necessary.

MAKES
18 ICE CUBES

TOTAL PREP &
COOKING TIME:
25–28 MINS

SWEDE, BROCCOLI & TURMERIC PUREE

200g (about ½) swede –
    peeled, cubed
100ml water
¼ tsp ground turmeric
70g broccoli – washed,
    cut into small florets

Two vitamin C powerhouses together in one meal –
swede and broccoli. Turmeric is earthy, bitter and
peppery in taste, and is believed to have anti-cancer
and anti-bacterial properties.

Place the swede in a saucepan with the water and
turmeric. Stir and simmer on low heat for 20–25 minutes
until tender.

While the swede is cooking, steam the broccoli florets
for 3–4 minutes until tender. Pop the steamed broccoli
and tender swede chunks into a food processor (or use
a handheld blender) and blend until smooth. Add cooled
boiled water or your baby's usual milk to thin out the
puree as necessary.

SWEET PEPPER GUACAMOLE PUREE

½ red pepper – washed, deseeded, chopped
½ ripe avocado – stone removed, roughly chopped
3 fresh coriander leaves
3–4 drops of fresh lime juice

~ TIP ~

For older kids spread this yummy guacamole on toast or serve with nachos for a fabulous after-school snack.

A little taste of Mexico. Avocado is a good source of healthy fats for you baby and peppers are sweet and rich in vitamin C and beta-carotene. Fresh coriander is a strong-tasting herb which complements the avocado and pepper beautifully.

Steam the pepper for 2½ minutes until tender. Pop the chopped avocado into a food processor (or use a handheld blender) along with the tender pepper, coriander leaves and lime juice. Blend until smooth, add cooled boiled water or your baby's usual milk to thin out the puree as necessary, then pass the puree through a sieve to remove unwanted red pepper skin before serving to your baby.

DREAMY BANANA PUREE (NO-COOK)

½ ripe banana – peeled, chopped
Pinch of ground nutmeg
1 tbsp baby's usual milk

Do you have a restless baby? The Vitamin B6 found in the bananas converts tryptophan into serotonin. Nutmeg has a sedative effect and calms the mind – it is widely used in Malaysia and India to promote sleep. I found this really helped to settle my baby.

Pop the banana into a bowl, add the nutmeg and milk and mash with a fork until smooth. Adjust the texture as necessary, with cooled boiled water or your baby's usual milk, to achieve the perfect consistency.

ZZZ'S SLEEPY CHERRY PORRIDGE ❄

20g porridge oats
150ml whole milk
4 saffron strands
2–3 sweet cherries –
    washed, stones
    removed

~ TIP ~

As an alternative,
replace the cherries with
apple puree (page 46)
and serve as a yummy,
floral-tasting apple
and saffron porridge.

Cherries and oats are a natural source of melatonin
which may encourage sleep. Saffron is reputed to
have mild sedative properties!

Place the oats in a saucepan along with the milk and
saffron. Bring to the boil gently on low heat and simmer
for 4–5 minutes until tender, stirring frequently. While
the porridge is simmering, steam the cherries until
tender.

Once the porridge is cooked, pop it into a food
processor (or use a handheld blender) along with the
tender cherries, and 1 tablespoon of your baby's usual
milk, and blend until smooth. Serve to baby warm. For
older babies, there's no need to puree the porridge –
texture is good.

MEAL PLAN — FOR WEEKS 2 & 3 OF PHASE 3

DAY	BREAKFAST	LUNCH
MONDAY	Vanilla rice with mango	Saag aloo puree
TUESDAY	Creamy tropical fruit puree	Sweet potato, coconut and lime
WEDNESDAY	Apricot puree with porridge	Butternut squash and cumin puree with rice
THURSDAY	Mango and apple puree* with full-fat Greek yogurt	Swede, cheese and chive puree
FRIDAY	Strawberry, basil and banana puree	Squashy dhal puree
SATURDAY	Strawberry, raspberry and blueberry puree with full-fat Greek yogurt	Swede, broccoli and turmeric puree
SUNDAY	Banana and cinnamon puree with porridge	Kiwi, mint and lime puree

DAY	BREAKFAST	LUNCH
MONDAY	Pear and cardamom puree with porridge	Sweet pepper guacamole puree
TUESDAY	Beetroot, apple and clove puree with full-fat Greek yogurt	Cauliflower and turmeric puree with rice
WEDNESDAY	Apricot and plum* puree with porridge	Carrot and parsnip puree* with rice
THURSDAY	Banana and avocado	Swede, broccoli and turmeric puree
FRIDAY	Vanilla rice with mango	Saag aloo puree
SATURDAY	Papaya, mango and orange puree with full-fat Greek yogurt	Avocado, papaya and cinnamon puree
SUNDAY	Apple and pear* puree with porridge	Swede, cheese and chive puree

*Create these purees by combining remaining ice-cubes from the first two weeks to save time and avoid wastage, or – if you have no leftover cubes of puree – see pages 40–49 (Stage 1 puree recipes). Offer your baby's usual milk or water to sip with meals.

STAGE 2 :
FLAVOUR
BLENDS AND TEXTURES
(7–9 MONTHS)
.....

As your little one continues to work her way up the stem of the flavour-led weaning flower, she's now ready for new and exciting flavour blends (more than one herb or spice in a meal), which will continue to help her little palate flourish. She'll also be ready for new, soft textures, and will be eating more nutrients so will continue to grow physically, too.

READY FOR STAGE 2 FLAVOUR-LED WEANING CHECKLIST:

☐ Enjoying two flavoursome meals a day

☐ Mixed ingredient purees with single flavours accepted

☐ Chewing motion may be starting to develop

TEXTURE

Super-smooth purees are no longer necessary. Now is the time to introduce new textures in the form of rougher purees, mashed food and soft lumps, to help your little one learn to chew. So get ready to work those arm muscles with your fork or masher. Don't be concerned if your little one hasn't cut her first teeth yet; her hard little gums will be able to power through soft lumps easily enough.

GOO-GOO, GA-GA

Your little one will most certainly be squealing, gurgling and babbling away – melting your heart with those cute little sounds. She may also be imitating speech sounds and saying words like 'mama' and 'dada'. This is the perfect age to help her develop her speech further, and chewing on soft lumps of food at mealtimes is a great way to do this.

Chewing is an essential motor skill for baby. It gives the jaw, lips and tongue muscles an excellent workout. Working these muscles regularly helps your little one develop speech, combining syllables to build word-like sounds with her cute little munchkin voice.

HOW MANY MEALS?

Your little one will probably be ready for three small meals a day (one meal = 2–3 ice-cubes, depending on appetite) and her meals will be growing bigger. You might find these months are also a good time to start offering snacks between meals if the meals are more than a few hours apart.

Snacks are best given in the form of finger foods, so your little one can practise hand-to-eye coordination and her grip. For some very simple first finger-food ideas, and more information on how to offer first finger foods safely, turn to page 126. See from page 128 for my finger food recipes. There is some further guidance on offering snacks on page 157 too.

FLEXIBLE ABOUT FLAVOURS

Before your little one reaches the 'picky eater's' phase, she will actually be very easy-going about trying out and tasting new foods and flavours. Get ready to GRAB this opportunity with both hands! This is the stage where you can introduce flavour blends into your little one's meals, and begin to broaden her palate. So stop fussy-eating behaviour before it's even begun, and get baby used to eating lots of different tastes and textures. By the time your little one becomes assertive about what she eats, she will be more likely to eat what you and the rest of the family are eating.

GROWTH SPURT ALERT!

You might feel that another growth spurt occurs around 9 months. Again, be prepared for a hungrier baby drinking more milk more frequently, irregular sleep patterns and a little fussiness for a few days.

MEAT AND FISH

It's time to introduce meat and fish as your little one's digestive system has further developed. Meat and fish, along with eggs and milk, are great sources of protein for your growing baby, as well as for a host of other nutrients. Protein is essential for healthy growth – not only does it build muscles, blood vessels and other organs, it also is required for the formation of hormones and parts of the immune system.

FANTASTIC FIRST FISH

White fish is mild in taste so makes a great first fish for baby. Cod, coley, pollack, haddock and tilapia are all great. You can then follow up with stronger-tasting oily fish rich in Omega-3 fatty acids – salmon, mackerel and sardines. Omega-3 is necessary for good brain function, nerve development, vision, general growth and development.

Fish is also excellent for cooking quick wholesome meals, making it perfect for busy parents! Just make sure you cook with skinless, boneless fillets. Double-check all the bones have been removed before serving.

Avoid fish containing high levels of mercury – shark, swordfish and marlin – as they can affect a baby's developing nervous system.

FIRST MEATS

As with fish, white meat is mild in taste, so poultry such as chicken or turkey makes an excellent first meat for baby. Once accepted, you can start introducing red meat such as lamb and beef. Rich in protein, zinc and iron, red meat is loaded with goodness for baby.

You should always cook with lean cuts of meat or lean minced meats as fat is not easy for baby to digest. Below are the cuts you might look to offer your little one:

* Chicken – skinless portions
* Turkey – skinless portions
* Lamb – casserole meat chunks, trimmed of excess fat
* Beef – casserole meat chunks, trimmed of excess fat

When preparing meat, it must be well cooked and first pureed, then mashed and then offered in lumps, as your baby learns how to chew.

VEGETARIAN PROTEIN SOURCES

If your little one is following a vegetarian diet there are plenty of good sources of protein for her as well. Eggs, milk, yogurt and other dairy sources are good options. Pulses, such as lentils, dried beans, soy foods, such as tofu, and nuts and seeds are also high in protein, and contribute valuable iron and zinc.

IRON

As mentioned, your little one's iron stores will start to run low from the age of 6 months. But you can boost levels by feeding her iron-rich foods. Good sources of iron include lean cuts of beef and lamb, dark chicken meat (legs and thighs), lentils, chickpeas, nuts, kidney beans and green vegetables (kale, broccoli and spinach in particular).

Aim to include at least one iron-rich food every day. Iron is absorbed easily into the body from meat but not so well from plant foods. You can boost this by teaming plant-based iron-rich dishes with foods rich in vitamin C (see page 24 for vitamin C-rich foods). For example, serve a spinach dish followed by my berry puree (see page 55).

MILK FEEDS

Baby's breastmilk or formula feeds will continue to slowly decrease as your baby gets more nutrition from solid foods. She should continue to take at least 500-600ml of formula or breastmilk per day to ensure she receives the necessary nutrients for healthy growth.

BANANA & CINNAMON PORRIDGE

20g porridge oats
150ml whole milk
Large pinch (⅛ tsp) of
    ground cinnamon
½ ripe banana –
    peeled, chopped

Sweet, woody cinnamon enhances the potassium-rich bananas, excellent for heart health and muscle growth, and energy-giving oats.

Place the oats in a saucepan with the milk. Bring to the boil gently on low heat and simmer for 4–5 minutes until tender. Once cooked, remove from the heat and pour into a bowl. Sprinkle over the cinnamon and scatter with the chopped banana. Stir to combine well and serve to baby warm.

CREAMY GREEN SPAGHETTI

20g spaghetti – broken into small pieces
½ ripe avocado – stone removed
2 basil leaves – fresh, washed, patted dry
8g medium Cheddar cheese – grated
½ tsp fresh lemon juice – ensure no seeds fall in
Pinch of garlic powder
1½ tbsp whole milk or your baby's usual milk

This is a great combination of flavours. Basil adds a lovely sweet, aniseed zing to the mild-tasting avocado, as well as being rich in vitamins and minerals. The cheese is a good source of protein, while the carb-rich spaghetti provides energy.

Cook the spaghetti according the the packet instructions.

Scoop out the avocado flesh and roughly chop it. Pop the chopped avocado into a food processor (or use handheld blender) along with the basil leaves, cheese, lemon juice, garlic powder and milk. Blend until creamy and smooth.

Drain the spaghetti, place in a bowl and add 1 tablespoon of the avocado sauce. Combine well, then add extra if necessary. The sauce is quite creamy so go easy on the amount you add, otherwise it may be too creamy for your little one. Chop the spaghetti pieces further or mash if necessary, and serve warm. Alternatively, offer to baby as a finger food. As baby grows, serve with a side of chopped cherry tomatoes.

The remaining sauce can be used for a playdate when friends come over, or you can eat it yourself with a little more seasoning, sprinkled with pine nuts and chopped cherry tomatoes. Yum!

TOTAL PREP &
COOKING TIME:
15 MINS

GARLICKY CAULIFLOWER & BROCCOLI CHEESE

100g broccoli – washed,
cut into small florets
100g cauliflower –
washed, cut into
small florets
20g unsalted butter
¼ tsp minced garlic
Pinch of ground cumin
1½ tbsp plain flour
130ml whole milk
Pinch of ground black
pepper
25g medium Cheddar
cheese – grated

~ TIP ~

Only freeze the meal
mashed. The whole
florets are better served
as a finger food when
freshly made.

Smooth, creamy and deliciously cheesy. This is packed
with cauliflower, broccoli and garlic – all good supporters
of the immune system.

Steam the broccoli and cauliflower until tender (popping
the cauliflower in the steamer after the broccoli has been
steaming for 2–3 minutes), then set aside to cool.

While the vegetables are steaming, melt the butter in a
saucepan on low heat, add the garlic and cumin and stir
for 30 seconds. Stir in the flour to form a paste (roux).
Start pouring in the milk a little at a time, whisking
vigorously to avoid any lumps forming. Once all of the
milk has been added, simmer until the sauce begins
to thicken.

Remove from the heat, add the black pepper and sprinkle
in the grated cheese. Stir until all the cheese has melted
and the sauce is smooth.

Add the sauce to the steamed veggies and mash as
required. Serve warm. Alternatively, leave the florets
whole and offer them to baby as a yummy finger food.
Excellent grip practice.

GUM-SOOTHING SQUASH ❄

250g (about ½) butternut squash – peeled, deseeded, cubed
Pinch of ground cloves
Pinch of ground cardamom
120g white cabbage – washed, drained, sliced

I've found this recipe good for helping to soothe uncomfortable teething pain. Cabbage is fibre-rich and a source of vitamin C.

Place the squash, cloves and cardamom in a saucepan with 5 tablespoons of water. Stir and simmer (covered) on low heat for 10–12 minutes (checking halfway through the cooking time) until tender.

While the squash is cooking, steam the cabbage for 5 minutes until completely tender, then pop it into a food processor (or use a handheld blender) along with the cooked squash. Blend using a pulse motion to retain some soft lumps and texture for baby. Remove any unwanted cabbage fibres and serve warm to baby.

BEETROOT & BROCCOLI MASH ❄️

100g (raw) beetroot –
    scrubbed, washed,
    peeled, sliced
80g broccoli – washed,
    cut into small florets
Pinch of ground turmeric
Pinch of ground black
    pepper

Beetroot may encourage the production of disease-fighting white blood cells and contains folic acid and iron. Broccoli is also rich in vitamin C while turmeric is known as an anti-inflammatory spice.

Steam the beetroot (8 minutes) and broccoli (3½ minutes) until tender. You can pop the broccoli in with the beetroot after 4–5 minutes. Pop the tender vegetables into a food processor (or use a handheld blender) along with the turmeric, black pepper and a little cooled boiled water if necessary. Blend using a pulse motion until you have a yummy textured mash for your little one.

TANGY APPLE DHAL ❄

1 tbsp olive oil
1 small onion – peeled, finely chopped
¼ tsp minced ginger
¼ tsp minced garlic
¼ tsp ground cinnamon
125g red lentils – soaked in water (10 mins), washed, drained
1 small sweet potato – washed, peeled, cubed
550ml water
1 sweet apple – peeled, cored, cut into small chunks

This dhal is an excellent source of protein – necessary for growth and repair of blood vessels, muscles and internal organs. Lentils and apples are also a source of dietary fibre, necessary for healthy little bowels.

Heat the oil in a saucepan on low heat, add the onion and sauté for 3–4 minutes, until soft and golden. Add the ginger, garlic and cinnamon and cook for a further 30 seconds.

Add the lentils to the pan along with the sweet potato, cover with the water and stir. Bring to the boil and simmer (uncovered) on medium heat for 20 minutes, until both the lentils and potato are tender.

While the lentils and potato are cooking, steam the apple chunks for 1½–2 minutes until tender then set aside. Add them to the curry once it's cooked, then stir and mash the whole curry to a consistency your little one will be comfortable eating. This is delicious served on its own or with rice or roti for toddlers.

ORANGE, DATE & SAFFRON RICE PUDDING

40g white basmati rice –
washed, drained
550ml whole milk
Pinch of saffron strands
20g soft dates – pitted,
finely chopped
Pinch of ground
cinnamon
¼ tsp orange zest

This aromatic, orange-infused rice pudding has a naturally sweet and floral taste. The dates are a concentrated source of energy for baby, fibre-rich (helping to keep bowels healthy), and provide small amounts of minerals, such as potassium.

Place the rice in a saucepan, pour in half of the milk, add the saffron and stir. Bring the milk to the boil gradually on low heat – this will take 5–10 minutes – then let it simmer (uncovered), stirring occasionally, until all of the milk has been absorbed by the rice. It will be thick and creamy.

While the rice is simmering, place the remaining milk in a blender (or use a handheld blender), add the dates and blend until smooth. Set aside.

Once the milk has been absorbed by the rice, remove the pan from the heat, mash the rice, then return to the heat and pour in the date and milk mixture, along with the cinnamon and orange zest. Stir and simmer (uncovered) on low heat for about 20 minutes, until the milk and mashed rice have combined into a rich, gooey consistency. If the consistency is too heavy, just add some extra milk and stir. Serve to baby warm.

COD WITH VANILLA SAUCE ❄

100ml whole milk
1 vanilla pod – split
   lengthways
Pinch of ground black
   pepper
½ tsp dried or freshly
   chopped chives
¼ tsp minced garlic
1 x 100g skinless, boneless
   cod fish fillet
30g frozen peas

~ TIP ~

As an alternative, place
this meal in a ramekin
dish, top with mashed
potatoes and pop it
under the grill to create
a yummy cod and vanilla
fish pie.

Cod and vanilla is a luxurious combination! Cod is
an excellent source of selenium (necessary for healthy
immune function), protein and vitamin B12. It is also a
mild-tasting fish, so an excellent first fish dish for baby.

Pour the milk into a saucepan, scrape out half the seeds
of the vanilla pod and add them to the milk, then add the
black pepper, chives and garlic. Stir and simmer on low
heat for 5 minutes to combine the flavours. You may need
to whisk the sauce to separate the vanilla seeds (to avoid
small clumps forming).

Pop the cod into the sauce and baste it with the
sauce, then allow to poach (covered) on low heat for
3–4 minutes before flipping it over, basting it again,
and letting it cook for a further 3–4 minutes until
the fillet is flaky and cooked through.

While the fish is poaching, steam the peas for 2 minutes
until tender and set aside.

Once the fillet is cooked through, break it into small
pieces (in the sauce), add the peas and stir. Blend or
mash as necessary without losing too much texture.
Serve to baby warm.

TILAPIA WITH MANGO & LIME SAUCE ❄

1 x 110g skinless, boneless
tilapia fillet or any
other white fish

Marinade:
1 tbsp olive oil
½ tsp minced garlic
1 tsp fresh lemon juice –
ensure no seeds fall in
Pinch of ground black
pepper

Mango sauce:
½ ripe mango – flesh
cubed
3 fresh coriander leaves
½ tsp fresh lime juice

**Sweet and yummy! This protein-rich fish dish is high in
a range of B vitamins and will go down a treat with your
little one.**

Preheat the oven to 200°C/400°F/gas mark 6. Combine
all the marinade ingredients in a bowl. Pop the fish fillet
into the bowl, ensuring it is covered with the marinade
and allow to marinate for 30 minutes.

Place the marinated fish on a large sheet of foil and
create a foil parcel by lifting the edges of the foil upwards
to the middle to create a point and fold the top edge.
Then fold the sides to seal the edges. You want to do this
to keep the steam inside the parcel. Place the parcel on a
baking tray and pop it in the oven for 10–11 minutes until
the fish is flaky and cooked through. Meanwhile, place
the mango, coriander and lime juice in a food processor
(or use a handheld blender) and blend until smooth.

Remove the fish from the oven and place it in a bowl
(do not add the cooking juices from the foil). Break the
fish into small pieces, pour the mango sauce over the
fish and combine well. Pop into a food processor (or use
a handheld blender) and blend to retain some texture.
Serve to baby warm on its own, or with steamed veg. For
older babies, serve with overcooked mushy basmati rice
(see page 60).

MOROCCAN CHICKEN COUSCOUS ❄

1 tbsp olive oil
½ onion – peeled, chopped
¼ tsp minced garlic
70g lean chicken
200ml low-salt stock
3g Medjool date – pitted, finely chopped
Pinch of ground coriander
Pinch of ground cumin
Pinch of ground cinnamon
7–8 drops of lemon juice
50g couscous
Flat-leaf parsley, for garnish – fresh, washed, chopped

~ TIP ~

The chicken can be frozen once cooked and cooled (before adding the couscous), but be sure to defrost and reheat the meal safely (see tips on defrosting and reheating on page 31).

Minced meat is always a great first meat for baby, as the meat has already been ground so is easier for her to munch on. This meal is a good mix of carbs (for energy) and protein.

Heat the oil in a saucepan and add the onion and garlic. Sauté for a few minutes until the onion is soft and golden, then add the mince and continue to sauté for up to 10 minutes, until cooked through, breaking up the mince with a spoon to avoid chunks from forming.

Add the stock, date, coriander, cumin, cinnamon and lemon juice, stir and bring to the boil, then add the couscous, stir and remove from the heat. Cover and allow the couscous to absorb the stock for 5–10 minutes.

Remove the lid and fluff up the couscous with a fork. The couscous should be a squishy consistency, making it easy for baby to eat and for you to mash further with a fork if necessary. Garnish with the parsley and serve to baby warm. Yummy!

ZINGY PINEAPPLE CHICKEN ❄

150ml unsweetened coconut milk (organic)
¼ tsp minced ginger
¼ tsp minced garlic
¼ tsp ground cumin
¼ tsp ground coriander
Pinch of ground black pepper
Pinch of ground turmeric
40g tinned pineapple – crushed
1 tbsp olive oil
180g chicken thigh (trimmed of fat) or 1 x skinless chicken breast fillet, both cubed
40g spinach leaves – washed

Cooking with chicken thigh meat (darker meat) means there will be higher levels of iron in this meal. The coriander aids digestion and cognitive function, and the pineapple and coconut provide the delicious flavours of the Caribbean!

Pour the coconut milk into a food processor and add the ginger, garlic, cumin, coriander, black pepper, turmeric and pineapple. Blend until smooth and set aside.

Heat the olive oil in a saucepan and add the chicken. Fry the chicken on low heat for a few seconds until sealed, then add the coconut sauce and simmer on low heat for a further 6–8 minutes until the chicken is tender and thoroughly cooked (if you're using thigh meat it may take a little longer to cook through than chicken breast).

While the chicken is cooking, steam the spinach. Add it to the saucepan when chicken is tender and cooked through, then pop the whole curry into a food processor (or use a handheld blender) and blend using a pulse motion to retain some soft lumps and texture for baby. Serve warm.

TOTAL PREP &
COOKING TIME:
18–20 MINS

MINI CHILLI CON CARNE ❄

1 tbsp olive oil
½ onion – peeled, finely chopped
100g lean beef or lamb mince
¼ tsp minced garlic
200g chopped tinned tomatoes
Pinch of ground cumin
Pinch of ground coriander
Pinch of ground black pepper
Pinch of ground turmeric
50g tinned kidney beans – rinsed and drained
10g dried apricot – finely chopped
30g red pepper – washed, deseeded, chopped
30g frozen broccoli florets – washed and chopped

Kidney beans and red meat are both excellent sources of protein and iron. The vitamin C from the broccoli and peppers make this meal extremely nutritious for your little one.

Heat the oil in a saucepan and add the onion. Sauté until the onion is soft and golden then add the mince and cook, stirring and breaking up the mince to avoid lumps, until the meat is opaque.

Remove the excess liquid then add the garlic, tomatoes, cumin, coriander, black pepper, turmeric, kidney beans, apricot and a splash of water, and simmer (covered) for 10 minutes.

Steam the pepper and broccoli for a few minutes and add to the pan of mince at the end. Combine well. Pop in a food processor (or use a handheld blender) and blend using a pulse motion to retain some soft lumps and texture for baby.

For older babies serve without blending alongside mushy overcooked rice (see page 60) and a dollop of soured cream.

LAMB & MINT CURRY ❄

1 tbsp olive oil
1 small onion – peeled,
    finely chopped
150g lean lamb cubes –
    fat trimmed
¼ tsp minced garlic
¼ tsp minced ginger
300ml water
1 tbsp natural yogurt
1 tsp tomato puree
Pinch of ground turmeric
Pinch of ground cumin
30g red pepper – washed,
    deseeded, chopped
4 small mint leaves –
    washed, finely
    chopped

Lamb and mint is a winning British flavour pairing
in this mild but flavoursome curry.

Heat the olive oil in a heavy-based casserole dish or
saucepan with a lid on medium heat. Add the onion,
lamb, garlic and ginger to the dish or pan and sauté
for a few minutes until the lamb is sealed, then stir in
the water, yogurt and tomato puree. Cook (covered) on
low heat for 1 hour 15 minutes until the lamb is tender.
Check halfway through and give it a stir. At the end
of the cooking time add the turmeric and cumin and
simmer (uncovered) for a further 5–10 minutes, until
the sauce thickens.

While the lamb is cooking, steam the pepper then
add it to the curry at the end along with the mint. Stir
to combine well, pop into a food processor (or use a
handheld blender) and blend using a pulse motion to
retain some soft lumps and texture for baby, adding
cooled boiled water if necessary.

MEAL PLAN – FOR STAGE 2

FROM 7 MONTHS	MORNING	LUNCH	EVENING
MONDAY	Vanilla rice with mango	Garlicky cauliflower and broccoli cheese	Banana and avocado puree
TUESDAY	Banana and cinnamon porridge	Moroccan chicken couscous	Saag aloo puree
WEDNESDAY	Orange, date and saffron rice pudding	Lamb and mint curry	Creamy tropical fruit puree
THURSDAY	Papaya, mango and orange puree with full-fat Greek yogurt	Tangy apple dhal	Cod with vanilla sauce
FRIDAY	Beetroot and broccoli mash	Saag aloo puree	Orange, date and saffron rice pudding
SATURDAY	Creamy tropical fruit puree	Cod with vanilla sauce	Garlicky cauliflower and broccoli cheese
SUNDAY	Apple and pear puree with porridge	Swede, cheese and chive puree	Beetroot and broccoli mash

Offer fruit purees and/or yogurt after each meal, along with water/formula or breastmilk to drink. Offer snacks between meals as your baby's appetite grows.

STAGE 2 AND 3:
FLAVOURFUL
FINGER FOODS
(7-12 MONTHS)

Until now I've focused on the spoon-feeding technique for your baby's flavour-led weaning journey. But finger foods are very much an integral part of the weaning process.

READY FOR FLAVOURED FINGER FOODS CHECKLIST:

☐ Baby is at least 7 months old (if younger, see opposite)

☐ Baby is grabbing for food or toys. If she can pick up toys, she can pick up food!

☐ Baby is exploring food with hands

☐ Baby is starting to use the thumb and forefinger to pick things up

INDEPENDENCE BEGINS

Finger foods are bite-sized or stick-shaped pieces of food babies can pick up with their podgy little fingers to feed themselves with, known as self-feeding. It is great for developing your little one's motor skills, hand to eye co-ordination and independence, so should be encouraged with lots of enthusiastic clapping and cheering from her parents.

TEXTURE

All finger foods should be soft and mush easily in the mouth. Remember some babies won't have teeth yet. As your little one grows and her chewing skill develops, she'll be able to tackle slightly firmer finger foods. By the time she is

12 months old, she'll be eating the same textures as the rest of the family.

SHAPE

Finger foods should be easy to pick up. Long shapes are good – steamed carrot sticks, for example, are easier for baby to wrap her little fingers around. Equally, bite-size chunks are good, too.

TASTE DISCOVERIES

Help your little one discover yummy tasting food through touch and feel. As you're well aware by now, babies naturally explore their world through their mouths and use it to make new discoveries. Everything goes in! So take advantage of your baby's natural instincts and offer her tasty flavoured finger foods. Yes, it will be messy, and your little one will no doubt mush food between her fingers, but this is all part of her exploring her sense of taste and touch. I'd recommend simply investing in some long-sleeved bibs and plastic floor mats (or throw down a towel for the floor), as things are going to get very messy from this point.

NO TEETH? NO PROBLEM!

If your little one hasn't cut any teeth yet, that's ok. You can still feed her finger foods provided they mush easily in the mouth. Aaliyah was a gummy baby until she was 10 months old and, even then, it was just the one tooth! But that didn't stop her! Babies' gums are actually quite hard, so they will be able to grind through soft textures easily enough.

WARNING – CHOKING HAZARD!

I cannot stress enough how important it is that you are always in the room supervising your little one when she is feeding herself. Fingers foods can be a very serious choking hazard. Don't offer whole nuts or popcorn, for example, always cut up foods like grapes, cherries and blueberries into small pieces, remember to cook vegetables first and avoid hard and unripened fruit and vegetables, like raw apple and raw carrot. Foods with skins (e.g. sausages) or bones (e.g fish) can also be a choking hazard. Remove stones, pips, skin and bones before feeding your baby. Please be careful and constantly watch your little one like a hawk!

FINGER FOODS FROM 6 MONTHS

You can offer finger foods from 6 months, alongside purees, but you'll still need to start with simple, basic foods to ensure first tastes are accepted. After that you can move onto flavoursome ones. For signs that your baby is ready for fingers foods, see page 36.

FIRST FINGER FOODS (FROM 6 MONTHS):

These should be very, VERY soft. So soft they disintegrate in a baby's mouth. Some good examples to try:

* Steamed broccoli florets (bites)
* Steamed cauliflower florets
* Steamed carrot sticks
* Ripe avocado slices
* Banana slices or sticks
* Steamed apple slices (no skin)
* Peach and plum bites (no skin)
* Plain boiled pasta shapes
* Simple steamed white fish

When you feel your little one is ready for more flavour and texture (from 7 months), continue with this chapter.

EASY CHEESY TURMERIC OMELETTE

1 tbsp olive oil
½ small onion – peeled, chopped
1 egg
1 tbsp whole milk
Pinch of ground black pepper
Pinch of ground turmeric
7g medium Cheddar cheese – grated

This protein- and calcium-rich breakfast is a great way for baby to start the day.

Heat the oil in a medium non-stick frying pan on medium-low heat, add the onion and sauté for 2 minutes until soft and golden. While the onion is cooking, crack the egg into a bowl, add the milk, black pepper, turmeric and cheese and whisk to combine.

Once the onion is cooked, reduce the heat to low and add the egg mixture to the pan. Lift and tilt the frying pan to spread the mixture evenly. Gently cook the egg on one side until brown, then flip it over to cook the other side. Once cooked remove from the pan. Cut into bite-size pieces or strips and serve to baby as a tasty finger food. For older babies, serve the omelette with roti or buttered wholemeal toast as a delicious breakfast.

TOTAL PREP &
COOKING TIME:
15 MINS

BANANA & COCONUT PANCAKES

100g plain flour
¼ tsp ground cinnamon
Pinch of ground allspice
1 egg
150ml whole milk
50ml unsweetened
   coconut milk (organic)
1 ripe banana – peeled,
   mashed
Unsalted butter, for frying

A yummy, fluffy finger food with a hint of allspice, which is believed to ease digestive discomfort. Great for breakfast, for baby and the whole family, served with a side of steamed apple slices or fruit of your choice.

Sift the flour into a bowl and fold in the cinnamon and allspice. Crack the egg into a separate bowl and whisk with the milk and coconut milk. Add the egg mixture to the flour gradually, whisking all the time (to avoid lumps). Add the mashed banana and whisk again until completely smooth.

Heat a knob of butter in a small non-stick frying pan (I like to use a 15cm frying pan), and add 2 tablespoons of the batter. Spread the batter evenly around the frying pan by lifting and tilting it, then cook on one side until golden. Flip it over, repeat for the other side and set aside once cooked through. Continue until all of the batter is used up.

MAKES
13 ICE-CUBES

TOTAL PREP & COOKING TIME:
15 MINS

PARSNIP YOGURT MEZZE ❄

1 tbsp olive oil
¼ tsp minced garlic
1 parsnip – washed, peeled, cored, chopped
1 sweet apple – washed, peeled, cored, chopped
1 tbsp full-fat Greek yogurt
Pinch of ground nutmeg
Pinch of ground black pepper

Similar to Greek tzatziki, this gorgeous, creamy, calcium-rich mezze will add lots of aromatic flavour to some soft finger foods.

Heat the olive oil in a saucepan, add the garlic, parsnip and apple and sauté on low heat for a few minutes, then add 2 tablespoons of water and let the apple and parsnip steam (covered) for 5–8 minutes (depending on the thickness of the pieces) until they are both tender.

Once tender, pop into a food processor (or use a handheld blender) and blend until smooth. Add the yogurt, nutmeg and black pepper and combine well. Spread over a very soft pitta slice (once your child has mastered soft finger foods) and cut into strips for your little one.

DATE & CINNAMON EGGY BREAD

1 egg yolk
150ml whole milk
2 dates – pitted, roughly
    chopped
Pinch of ground
    cinnamon
2 slices of white bread –
    crusts cut off
2 knobs of unsalted butter

~ TIP ~

For older kids and adults
serve the eggy bread
with freshly chopped
ripe bananas sautéed
in a little brown sugar.

Soft, delicious and fluffy – eggy bread is excellent
for breakfast. Dates are super nutritious and a source
of iron. They are also a healthy source of fibre. Their
sweetness and honey-like flavour are an added bonus.

Place the egg yolk, milk, dates and cinnamon in a food
processor (or use a handheld blender) and blend until
smooth. Pour the mixture into a dish large enough to
dip a slice of bread in.

Place one slice of bread in the dish, face down, and let
it soak for a few seconds without becoming too soggy.
Turn it over and repeat on the other side.

Heat a knob of butter in a frying pan on medium heat
and gently place the slice of bread in. Cook for a few
minutes until golden brown and flip to cook the other
side for a further few minutes.

Once thoroughly cooked (but not tough or hard),
remove the eggy bread from the pan and cut it into
strips or bite-size pieces. Repeat for the second slice
of bread and serve to baby warm on its own or with
freshly cut fruit of your choice.

MAKES
8 DINNER-PLATE-
SIZED ROTIS

TOTAL PREP &
COOKING TIME:
40–50 MINS

SPICY SPINACH ROTI BITES/THEPLA

200g atta/chapatti flour,
    plus extra for dusting
¼ tsp ground turmeric
¼ tsp ground coriander
¼ tsp ground cumin
Pinch of ground ginger
½ tsp garlic powder
25g spinach leaves –
    washed, roughly torn
    into pieces (no stems)
1 tbsp vegetable oil
120ml hot water
Unsalted butter, to serve

These bites are an excellent energy-boosting meal for your little one. Spinach contains good levels of vitamin K, necessary for blood-clotting, and vitamin A, vital for good immune-system function. Give this to your baby once they have mastered soft finger foods.

Place the flour in a bowl along with the spices and torn spinach, and stir to combine. Make a well in the centre of the flour and pour the oil into the well. Start adding the water around the side of the well, a little at a time, and stir until a dough begins to form. You may not need all of the water as spinach contains a lot of water. If the dough is slightly too sticky (from too much water being added) add some extra flour to make the dough manageable. Remove the dough ball from the bowl and knead it for 1–2 minutes on a floured surface.

Divide the dough into 8 pieces and shape each piece into a small round ball. Sprinkle some flour over the worksurface and rolling pin so the dough doesn't stick and roll one of the balls until it resembles a 25cm round pancake. Repeat this process for all the dough balls.

Heat a large frying pan or thava (round, flat frying pan) on medium heat and cook one roti for 2–3 minutes until bubbles appear on the surface and the roti begins to brown. Turn it over and cook until bubbles appear on the other side. Then flip the roti at regular intervals until it begins to puff up. Remove and set aside. Repeat for all the rotis.

Once cooked, spread a little unsalted butter over the fresh roti, cut into strips and serve immediately whilst still warm. Alternatively, you can freeze the cooked rotis for later.

For plain chapattis, which are also a great finger food for older babies, leave out the spices and spinach and follow the same method.

CHEWABLE TEETHING STICKS

½ tbsp olive oil
¼ tsp ground cinnamon
Pinch of ground nutmeg
1 small sweet potato –
    washed, peeled, cut
    into 1cm-thick sticks

If your little one is teething, this tasty snack may help to soothe those sore gums. The nutmeg not only provides a warm, aromatic taste to complement the sweet potato, it also contains the compound 'eugenol', which is used as a natural medicine to treat toothaches. Combined with the powerful analgesic properties of cinnamon, this is a wonderful snack to combat teething pains.

Preheat the oven to 200°C/400°F/gas mark 6.

Place the oil, cinnamon and nutmeg in a bowl and stir. Add the potato sticks and give them a good toss to coat them with the seasoning. Lay them flat on a foil-covered baking tray and place on the middle shelf of the oven.

Bake for 15–20 minutes or until tender, turning them over halfway. Allow to cool before serving to baby.

BROCCOLI FRITTATA WITH BASIL

40g white potato –
washed, peeled, cut
into small cubes
40g frozen broccoli florets
– washed, chopped
2 eggs
¼ tsp minced garlic
1 tablespoon whole milk
Pinch of ground black
pepper
Pinch of ground turmeric
2 basil leaves – fresh,
washed, finely
chopped
Olive oil, for frying
Small handful grated
medium Cheddar
cheese

An easy Italian classic with yummy hints of basil coming
through. High in vitamin C and protein, this meal is
excellent for healthy growth, and for babies who are
following a vegetarian diet.

Preheat the grill to medium.

Steam the broccoli florets and potato cubes until tender
and set aside: the potatoes will need longer to cook, so
steam them for 4 minutes first, before adding the broccoli
and steaming for another 4 minutes.

Lightly whisk the eggs in a bowl with the garlic, milk,
black pepper, turmeric and basil until combined, then
heat a little oil in a non-stick frying pan on medium-low
heat and pour in the mixture. Spread the mixture evenly
by lifting the frying pan and tilting it, then sprinkle over
the broccoli and potato. Cook for betweem 30 seconds
and 1 minute, until the bottom is well cooked and firm,
then sprinkle the cheese over the top and pop it under
the grill to brown for 2–3 minutes. Cut into pieces for
your baby and serve warm.

MAKES
3–4
SERVINGS

TOTAL PREP &
COOKING TIME:
25–30 MINS

INDIAN ROASTED SWEDE STICKS

½ tbsp olive oil
¼ tsp minced garlic
Pinch of ground turmeric
Large pinch (1/8 tsp) of
    ground garam masala
130g swede – washed,
    peeled, cut into
    1cm sticks

Offer this from 10 months+. Influenced by India, this mild sweet and savoury flavour combination is fab! Garam masala is particularly beneficial. It's the Indian equivalent of Italian mixed herbs. With so many anti-inflammatory spices in one spice blend, your little one will reap multiple health benefits from this snack.

Preheat the oven to 200°C/400°F/gas mark 6.

Place the oil, garlic, turmeric and garam masala in a bowl and stir. Add the swede sticks to the bowl and give them a good toss to coat them in the seasoning. Lay them flat on a foil-covered baking tray and place on the middle shelf of the oven.

Bake for 10–15 minutes or until tender, turning over halfway. Allow to cool before serving to baby.

BEETROOT SEEKH KEBAB ❄

150g lean beef or lamb mince, finely ground
¼ tsp ground cumin
¼ tsp ground coriander
¼ tsp ground garam masala
¼ tsp ground turmeric
½ tsp minced garlic
2 tbsp fresh mint leaves – washed, finely chopped
15g (raw) beetroot – scrubbed, washed, peeled, finely chopped, steamed
1 tsp plain full-fat yogurt
Olive oil, for brushing

~ TIP ~

Don't be alarmed if there's a lot of pink/red juice. It isn't blood from the meat, it's beetroot juice!

Our good friend garam masala is back on the menu, providing your little one with its many health benefits – boosting immunity, preventing indigestion and boosting cognitive function. This finger food is also rich in iron and protein.

Place the mince, cumin, coriander, garam masala, turmeric, garlic, mint, steamed beetroot (fully cooked) and yogurt in a bowl and combine well. Shape into 1cm-wide fingers and chill in the fridge for 30 minutes before cooking. If you want to freeze them, wrap each kebab individually in cling film and pop them in the freezer.

To cook the kebabs, heat a griddle pan on medium heat or preheat the grill. Brush the kebabs with a little olive oil and cook on a griddle pan, or on a tray under a grill, until cooked through, tender and the juices run clear. Allow to cool and cut into smaller bite-size pieces. Serve with my Pear, mint and coriander chutney (page 149) as a yummy dip.

MAKES
2–3
PIZZAS

CHEESY TORTILLA PIZZA SLICES ❄

Pizza sauce:
200g tinned plum
   tomatoes
5g dried apricot –
   finely chopped
½ tsp minced garlic
¼ tsp dried oregano
Pinch of ground black
   pepper

Pizza base:
2–3 mini tortilla wraps –
   white or wholemeal
15g medium Cheddar
   cheese – grated

~ TIP ~
Add chopped peppers,
chopped mushrooms and
sweetcorn kernels and
transform this finger food
into a quick and filling
after-school snack for
older children.

Offer this from 10 months+. These pizza slices are
perfect finger food for baby. Soft, nutritious, easy to
pick up and yummy! The apricot in the sauce adds an
extra zing of flavour, and oregano offers an earthy taste
has spicy undertones, and not only does it add a lot
of flavour to meals, it can also help protect baby
against nausea and asthma. The sauce freezes well.

Preheat the grill to medium-low.

Pop the tomatoes and apricot in a food processor
and blend until smooth, then pour into a saucepan
and add the garlic, oregano and black pepper. Simmer
on medium-low heat for 6–8 minutes, until the sauce
has thickened. Set aside.

Lay the tortilla on a foil-covered baking tray and spread
2–3 tablespoons of pizza sauce evenly over the tortilla.
Sprinkle over the grated cheese and pop it under the
grill until the cheese has melted and is bubbling (this
will only take a minute or two, so keep your eye on it).
Remove from the grill, then cut into triangles. Leave
to cool before serving to baby.

MAKES
6 FISH
FINGERS

TOTAL PREP &
COOKING TIME:
30 MINS

HOMEMADE DILL FISH FINGERS ❄

1 x 145g skinless, boneless cod fillet (or any other firm white fish)
25g plain flour
¼ tsp ground black pepper
¼ tsp ground turmeric
Pinch of ground mild paprika
1 slice of white bread – a few days old, blended into breadcrumbs
1 tbsp freshly chopped dill
1 egg – beaten
Olive oil, for brushing

～ TIPS ～

* If you wish, add a drop of lemon juice to the fish finger pieces before serving to enhance the citrusy flavour of the dill.

* Try serving the fish fingers alongside my Pea and mint puree (page 67) as a yummy dip. For older kids or adults serve the fish fingers with a garlic mayo dip.

Offer this from 10 months+. Dill, an aromatic, bitter and citrusy herb, is perfect with fish. Dill also has antioxidant and anti-bacterial properties and can be useful in preventing coughs.

Preheat the oven to 200°C/400°F/gas mark 6.

Using a sharp knife, cut the cod fillet into stick shapes about 1.5cm wide.

Place the flour in a bowl and season with the black pepper, turmeric and paprika. Stir to combine. Place the breadcrumbs in another bowl, add the dill and toss until well combined. Put the beaten egg in a third bowl.

Coat the fish sticks in the seasoned flour, then dip in the egg and toss into the breadcrumbs, making sure the fish is well coated. Repeat for all the fish sticks. If you will be freezing the fish fingers, freeze them at this point (before cooking).

To cook, place them on a lightly greased or greaseproof paper-lined baking tray and brush the fish fingers with a little olive oil. Pop them in the oven for 10 minutes until cooked, turning over halfway through. Remove from the oven, allow to cool and cut into bite-size pieces before serving to baby.

TROPICAL JERK SALMON

1 tsp olive oil
Pinch of ground cloves
Pinch of dried thyme
Pinch of ground cinnamon
Pinch of ground nutmeg
Pinch of ground allspice
¼ tsp minced ginger
¼ tsp minced garlic
20g tinned pineapple – drained, crushed
½ dried apricot, roughly chopped
1 x 110g boneless salmon fillet

Offer this from 10 months+. Salmon is an oily fish rich in Omega-3 fatty acids, vitamin B12, vitamin D and protein. So getting some yummy salmon into your little one's diet is a must! The juicy pineapple is rich in vitamin C and adds a mild sweetness to the dish, along with the dried apricot.

Preheat the oven to 200°C/400°F/gas mark 6.

Place the oil, cloves, thyme, cinnamon, nutmeg, allspice, ginger, garlic, pineapple and apricot in a food processor or blender and blend until smooth. Spread the marinade over the salmon fillet and place the fillet on a long piece of foil. Create a foil parcel by lifting the edges of the foil upwards to the middle to create a point and fold the top edge. Then fold the sides to seal the edges. You want to do this to keep the steam inside the parcel.

Place the foil parcel on a baking tray and place the tray on the middle shelf of the oven to cook for 15–18 minutes, until flaky and tender. Remove from the oven and allow to stand for a few minutes, then unwrap the parcel and allow the salmon to cool. Serve to baby in small mashed, bite-size chunks, ensuring you have removed the skin. For babies with larger appetites, or for toddlers, serve alongside basmati rice and freshly steamed peas.

MAKES
9–10
CHICKEN STRIPS

TOTAL PREP &
COOKING TIME:
35–38 MINS

PERI PERI CHICKEN STRIPS ❄

½ tsp ground mild
  paprika
1 tbsp fresh lemon juice –
  ensure no seeds fall in
½ tsp minced garlic
½ tsp minced ginger
½ red pepper – washed,
  deseeded, chopped
1 tbsp olive oil
1 chicken breast fillet
  (skinless) – cut
  into strips

Offer this from 10 months+. Lovely savoury-tasting chicken strips for baby, these are rich in protein and have a boost of vitamin C.

Place the paprika, lemon juice, garlic, ginger, red pepper and olive oil in a food processor or blender and blend until you have a smooth sauce. Smear the sauce over the chicken strips in a bowl, ensuring all pieces are covered, and set aside for 30 minutes to marinate, allowing the flavours to develop. If you want to freeze the strips, freeze them wrapped individually in cling film at this stage (before cooking).

To cook the chicken strips, heat a griddle pan on medium heat or preheat the grill. Cook the strips on the griddle or on a tray under the grill until tender. You can check by piercing the chicken to ensure it is no longer pink. Allow to cool and serve with my yummy Lemon and herb dip (page 150).

DIPS, CHUTNEYS & SPREADS

Transform a boring finger food simply by adding a yummy dip to your little one's tray. Serve these dips with soft steamed fruit and vegetables for younger babies or plain cooked chicken strips or roti for those who have mastered finger food.

**MAKES
4 SERVINGS**

PEAR, MINT & CORIANDER CHUTNEY

1 ripe pear – washed, peeled, cored, roughly chopped

Handful of mint leaves – fresh, washed

Handful of coriander leaves – fresh, washed

Pears are a good source of vitamin C and fibre – great for keeping baby 'regular'. This is a very light, fresh-tasting dip which can be offered with many different finger foods, such as steamed vegetables, fish or kebabs.

Place the pear and herbs in a food processor or blender (or use a handheld blender) and blend to form a paste. Serve to baby with a finger food of your choice.

The chutney can be kept in an airtight container in the fridge for up to 2 days.

MAKES
2–3
SERVINGS

MAKES
2–3
SERVINGS

TOTAL PREP &
COOKING TIME:
2–3 MINS
PLUS 1 HOUR TO SET

LEMON & HERB DIP (NO-COOK)

Fragrant, light and citrusy, this dip works beautifully alongside my Peri Peri Chicken Strips (page 148).

2 tbsp crème fraîche
½ tsp fresh lemon juice
½ tsp washed and finely chopped fresh dill
Pinch of black pepper

Simply combine all the ingredients in a bowl. The dip can be kept in an airtight container in the fridge for up to 2 days.

HERBY PEAR BUTTER (NO-COOK)

Pears are mild and sweet. Put them in butter with a hint of aromatic rosemary, and you've got an unusual yet winning flavour combination.

50g unsalted butter, at room temperature, roughly chopped
1 tbsp pureed pear (page 46)
1 tsp washed and finely chopped fresh rosemary needles

Place all the ingredients in a food processor (or use a handheld blender) and blend until combined. Transfer the herby pear butter to an airtight container and place in the fridge to set (for around 1 hour). Spread on fingers of bread, toast or pitta for a burst of flavour. It will keep in the fridge for up to 3 days.

SWEET & SOUR PLUM CHUTNEY

2 plums – washed,
    stoned, peeled, sliced
10g sultanas
¼ tsp ground cinnamon
Pinch of ground nutmeg
Pinch of ground ginger
90ml water

This chutney smells just like Christmas! Stunning, fragrant flavours – cinnamon, nutmeg and ginger – all complement the flavour of the plums beautifully.

Place the plums, sultanas, cinnamon, nutmeg and ginger in a saucepan, pour in the water and bring to the boil. Reduce the heat and simmer (covered) for 15 minutes until the plums are tender, stirring occasionally. Transfer to a food processor (or use a handheld blender) and blend until smooth. It can be kept in an airtight container in the fridge for up to 2 days.

CUCUMBER RAITA (NO-COOK)

2 tbsp full-fat Greek
  yogurt
2 fresh mint leaves
Tiny pinch of ground
  cumin
Tiny pinch of ground
  ginger
2.5cm piece of cucumber,
  washed, peeled,
  deseeded

A fresh cucumber raita. The cumin and ginger also help with a healthy digestive tract. Try serving it alongside my Lamb and mint curry on page 121 or my Chicken kofta curry on page 211.

Place all of the ingredients in a food processor (or use a handheld blender) and blend until smooth.

Serve straight away.

CREAMY SARDINE SPREAD (NO-COOK)

1 boneless sardine from a
   tin (in water) – drained
2 tbsp full-fat soft cheese
Pinch of ground mild
   paprika
Pinch of dried parsley

A stronger-tasting spread, rich in vitamin B12, selenium, Omega-3 fatty acids, vitamin D, calcium and protein. So as you can see, there are many benefits to smearing some of this spread on your little one's finger food.

Place all the ingredients in a food processor (or use a handheld blender) and blend until smooth and well combined. Spread over bread, toast, pitta or serve as a yummy dip for vegetables. It will keep in an airtight container in the fridge for up to 2 days.

STAGE 3: CHUNKIER MEALS AND NEW FLAVOUR BLENDS (10–12 MONTHS)

The flavour-led weaning flower bud is now half open. Not long to go before your little one's palate has fully flourished. Exciting!

By now your baby should already be appreciating the taste of good food. Don't stop now. Keep the variety coming with lots of new recipes and flavour combinations found in this chapter. She'll also be pretty good at tackling those soft lumps, so it's time to make meals chunkier than before, to help further develop her chewing ability and speech.

Your little one is also just one feeding stage away from big family meals, and these recipes reflect that. Now you'll be transitioning her over to meals that are more adult-like and complete. For example, rice with curry and bolognaise with spaghetti. Up until now, most foods have been mashed into one bowl. Now elements can be kept separate and served together, so your little one can begin to appreciate how different flavours, textures and accompaniments can work together to create even more flavoursome and interesting meals.

READY FOR FLAVOUR-LED WEANING STAGE 3 CHECKLIST:

☐ 10 months of age

☐ Devouring three small meals a day and some snacks

☐ Baby's grip is stronger and she is able to hold a spoon to clumsily feed herself

☐ Enjoying stage 2 meals and finger foods

☐ Soft lumps are a doddle! Proper chewing is now on the agenda.

☐ Baby is drinking from a sippy cup or free-flow beaker

FLAVOUR VARIETY

A baby's taste will regularly change and 'favourite meals' will begin to shine through from this age so variety is key. New flavour blends and recipes create a whole new range of tastes for baby. The different flavour blends will work together to create even more delicious meals for your little one.

TEXTURE

Meals are chunkier and can now be chopped and shredded instead of mashed. Depending on your little one's development, mashed meals and soft lumps may still be required at the beginning of this stage. But it is a good idea to move on as quickly as your baby is able to avoid getting stuck at this stage. Food should still be soft. No hard lumps.

MILK FEEDS

Baby's breastmilk or formula feeds will continue to slowly decrease as your baby gets more nutrition from solid foods. She should continue to take at least 500-600ml of formula or breastmilk per day to ensure she receives the necessary nutrients for healthy growth.

APPETITE AND ENERGY LEVELS

* Appetites vary from baby to baby but on average your little one should be ready for three healthy meals and two snacks per day.

* By now your little one will likely be crawling, rolling and possibly cruising too, so snacks are important for keeping energy levels up.

* Two snacks a day (one between each meal), will be enough to keep your little one on the move. High-energy snacks are those that are rich in complex carbohydrates, such as roti, pitta bread and toast. Also offer choices from other food groups, such as cheese and chopped soft fruit, for variety.

* At mealtimes the average portion size for a 10-month-old baby should be one baby weaning bowl. As a guide, you could aim for meals to be one third starchy foods, one third protein-rich and one third fruit and vegetables, plus some dairy foods as well.

FRUITY BREKKIE PORRIDGE — PLENTY OF WAYS!

Porridge is a fab way for baby to start the day. Great for energy and heart health, it is also fibre-rich, and fibre is key for healthy little bowels.

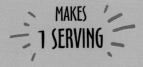

MAKES
1 SERVING

PLUM CHUTNEY PORRIDGE

20g porridge oats
150ml whole milk
1 tbsp Sweet and sour
   plum chutney
   (see page 151)

Vitamin C-rich plum chutney is excellent for maintaining immunity. The vitamin K content also contributes towards healthy bones.

~~~~~~

Place the oats in a saucepan with the milk and gently bring to the boil on low heat. Simmer for 4–5 minutes until the oats are tender.

Once cooked, remove the porridge from the heat and pour it into a bowl. Add the sweet and sour plum chutney and stir to combine. Serve to baby warm.

PEANUT BUTTER & JAM PORRIDGE

20g porridge oats
150ml whole milk
60g ripe strawberries –
  washed, hulled, sliced
15g Medjool date – pitted,
  finely chopped
½ tsp smooth peanut
  butter

~ TIP ~

Increase the amount of
peanut butter, or reduce
the amount of strawberry
'jam', according to taste.
You can also leave out the
peanut butter altogether
and serve it as a strawberry
'jam' porridge.

This porridge is yummy as long as your little one isn't
allergic to peanuts. Peanuts are chock-full of healthy
fats, protein and potassium. Combined with iron-rich
dates, and strawberries rich in vitamin C and fibre,
this classic American combo is super nutritious.

Place the oats in a saucepan with the milk and gently
bring to the boil on low heat. Simmer for 4–5 minutes
until the oats are tender.

While the porridge is simmering, place the strawberries
and date in a food processor or blender and blend until
smooth, then set aside, passing it through a sieve to
remove the little strawberry seeds if you like (though
this isn't necessary).

Once the porridge is cooked, remove it from the heat and
pour into a bowl. Swirl the peanut butter into the porridge
while it's still warm, then top with the strawberry 'jam'.
Serve to baby warm.

MAKES
6 SMALL
SERVINGS

TOTAL PREP &
COOKING TIME:
35 MINS

MUSHROOM & BROCCOLI RISOTTO ❄

1½ tbsp olive oil
1 small onion – peeled, chopped
¼ tsp minced ginger
½ tsp minced garlic
120g mushrooms – washed, stems removed, caps sliced and cut into small pieces
700ml hot low-salt vegetable stock
Pinch of ground nutmeg
Pinch of ground cumin
Pinch of ground black pepper
100g arborio risotto rice – washed, drained
60g broccoli florets – washed, chopped
½ tsp full-fat soft cheese, to serve (optional)

The soft texture of cooked mushrooms means they are perfect for further aiding your little one's chewing skills. They are also very much savoury in taste. Nutritionally, mushrooms are a source of a range of B vitamins.

Heat the oil in a saucepan on medium-low heat, add the onion and sauté for 4–5 minutes until soft and golden. Add the ginger, garlic and mushrooms with a splash of water and sauté until the mushrooms soften and any liquid has evaporated, then add the stock, nutmeg, cumin, black pepper and rice. Stir and bring to the boil then simmer (covered) on low heat for 15–20 minutes until the rice is creamy and tender.

While the rice is cooking, steam the broccoli florets until tender. Stir them into the cooked risotto and remove a serving for your little one. Stir in the soft cheese, if using, for extra creamy richness and serve to baby warm.

If freezing, separate the cooled risotto into individual portions and pop them in small airtight containers or resealable freezer bags, ensuring the air has been squeezed out of the bags. See page 31 for defrosting and reheating guidelines.

~ TIP ~

Pop some cooked boneless (unsmoked) mackerel pieces in the risotto to add extra oily fish health benefits.

TOTAL PREP &
COOKING TIME:
35–40 MINS

CURRIED LENTILS WITH SQUASH ❄

2 tbsp olive oil
1 onion – peeled, chopped
1 tsp minced garlic
1 tsp minced ginger
200g tinned chopped
    tomatoes
½ tsp ground garam
    masala
½ tsp mild curry powder
90g red lentils – soaked
    in cold water (10 mins),
    washed, drained
½ butternut squash –
    peeled, deseeded, cut
    into 2.5cm chunks
60g dried apricots,
    finely chopped
550ml water
Cooked quinoa, roti
    (see page 134) or rice
    (see page 60), to serve

Rich in beta-carotene (a form of vitamin A), this meal promotes healthy eyes, skin and immune system. The dried apricots are a source of iron, and lentils are a good source of protein and iron, so this meal is great for veggie babies.

Heat the oil in a saucepan on medium-low heat, add the onion and sauté for 5 minutes until soft and golden, then add the garlic and ginger and sauté for a further 30 seconds to 1 minute. Add the tomatoes, garam masala and curry powder and sauté for a further 2 minutes to lightly cook the spices.

Add the lentils, squash, apricots and water, and stir. Bring to the boil and simmer (covered) on medium-low heat for 20–25 minutes until the lentils are cooked and the squash is tender and breaks apart easily. Serve with quinoa, roti or rice.

MAKES
4 SMALL
SERVINGS

TOTAL PREP &
COOKING TIME:
25 MINS

ORANGE CHICKEN KORMA ❄

1 tbsp olive oil
1 small onion – peeled, chopped
1 whole clove
1 whole green cardamom pod
1 tsp minced garlic
1 tsp minced ginger
½ tsp ground garam masala
½ tsp ground cumin
½ tsp ground coriander
100ml water
3 tbsp full-fat Greek yogurt
¼ tsp ground turmeric
1 tsp tomato puree
1 chicken breast fillet (skinless) – cut into cubes
1 tbsp freshly squeezed orange juice – ensure no seeds fall in
Small handful of fresh coriander leaves
Overcooked mushy rice or roti, to serve

No weaning cookbook would be complete without a chicken korma recipe! The mildest tasting curry of all, with a hint of citrusy orange combined with all those lovely aromatic spices, this curry is a real treat for baby.

Heat the oil in a saucepan on medium-low heat, add the onion, clove and cardamom pod and sauté until the onion is soft and golden, then add the garlic, ginger, garam masala, cumin and ground coriander and sauté for a further 1–2 minutes. Add the water, yogurt, turmeric and tomato puree then simmer on low heat, stirring frequently, for 5 minutes until the sauce begins to thicken.

Add the chicken to the sauce and cook on low heat for 7–8 minutes then check if the chicken is cooked through. If not, cook for a little longer.

Once the chicken is cooked and tender, remove and discard the cardamom pod and clove. Remove from the heat and stir in the orange juice and a sprinkling of fresh coriander leaves. Chop or mash, as required, and serve to baby warm with overcooked mushy rice or with roti.

THAI CHICKEN CURRY ❄️

1½ tbsp olive oil
1 onion – peeled, chopped
½ tsp minced garlic
½ tsp minced ginger
¼ tsp ground turmeric
¼ tsp ground cumin
1 tomato – washed
150ml unsweetened
  coconut milk (organic)
1 tbsp fresh lemon juice –
  ensure no seeds fall in
½ lemongrass stalk –
  trimmed, dry outer
  layers removed, tender
  core bashed
¼ tsp ground garam
  masala
1 chicken breast fillet
  (skinless) – cut into
  cubes
60g green beans – washed,
  trimmed, cut into
  2.5cm lengths
Overcooked mushy rice
  (see page 60), to serve

A taste of yummy Thai cuisine for baby. The green beans in this curry are an excellent source of vitamin K, thought to play a role in building strong bones and assisting in blood clotting to heal wounds. Exactly what your little one will need when running around.

~~~~~~~

Heat the oil in a saucepan on low heat, add the onion and sauté for 3–4 minutes until soft and golden. Add the garlic, ginger, turmeric and cumin, grate in the tomato, and allow the spices to cook for 30 seconds to 1 minute. Add the coconut milk, lemon juice, lemongrass and garam masala and simmer on low heat for 5–6 minutes until the sauce begins to thicken.

Add the chicken pieces to the sauce, stir and simmer gently for 6–8 minutes or until the chicken is tender and no longer pink inside. While the chicken is cooking, steam the green beans for 5–6 minutes until tender and set aside.

Once the chicken is fully cooked, remove the lemongrass stalk and add the green beans. Combine well, mash or chop as required, and serve warm with overcooked mushy rice for your little one, or why not give noodles a go? For grown-ups, serve with yummy coconut rice and a wedge of lime.

SAUCY SARDINES ❄

1 tbsp olive oil
1 small onion – peeled, chopped
1 tsp minced garlic
200g tinned plum tomatoes – roughly chopped
Pinch of ground black pepper
½ tsp ground garam masala
½ tsp fresh lemon juice
40g tinned boneless sardine fillets (in water) – drained
2 fresh basil leaves – roughly torn
Freshly cooked pasta, to serve

Rich in antioxidant lycopene, vitamin C, protein and Omega-3 fatty acids, this sauce is a nutritional powerhouse. The garlic, basil and garam masala work together to give this yummy sauce a distinct and unique flavour.

Heat the oil in a saucepan on medium-low heat, add the onion and sauté until soft and golden, then add the garlic and sauté for a further minute. Pour in the chopped tomatoes, add the black pepper, garam masala and lemon juice, and simmer for 5–6 minutes until the sauce begins to thicken.

Roughly chop or mash the sardines, add them to the sauce, stir and cook for a further few minutes. Turn off the heat, sprinkle over the torn basil and stir through to combine. Add 1–2 tablespoons of sauce to some freshly cooked pasta. Serve warm. Freeze the remaining sauce for another day.

TOTAL PREP &
COOKING TIME:
25 MINS

CREAMY MASALA SALMON PASTA ❄

Tomato masala:
1 tbsp olive oil
½ onion – peeled,
    chopped
½ tsp minced garlic
1 tomato – washed,
    chopped
½ tsp ground cumin

White sauce:
2 tbsp unsalted butter
2 tbsp plain flour
250ml low-salt fish or
    vegetable stock
Pinch of ground black
    pepper
100g boneless, skinless
    salmon from a tin (in
    spring water), drained
50g frozen peas
Freshly cooked pasta,
    to serve

Rich in vitamins D and B12, this is a yummy, nutritious
meal. The cumin provides smoky undertones and is
good for soothing indigestion and boosting immunity.

To make the tomato masala, heat the oil in a frying pan
on medium heat, add the onion and sauté for 2 minutes
until soft and golden. Add the garlic, tomato and cumin
and sauté for a few minutes until the tomato begins to
soften, then remove from the heat and set aside.

To make the white sauce, melt the butter in a saucepan
on low heat, then add the flour. Stir continuously to form
a paste (roux), then pour in the stock a little at a time,
whisking vigorously to avoid any lumps forming. Once all
of the stock has been incorporated, add the black pepper
and tomato masala and flake in the salmon, using your
fingers to ensure there are no sneaky bones left in the
fish. Simmer (uncovered) on low heat for 5–6 minutes,
stirring occasionally, until the sauce begins to thicken.

Meanwhile, steam the peas for 2½–3 minutes until tender
(or place the peas in a saucepan with 2 tablespoons of
water and simmer, covered, on low heat).

Pop the cooked peas into the salmon sauce, mash or
chop as required, and serve the creamy masala salmon
with a portion of cooked pasta.

MAKES
6 SMALL
SERVINGS

TOTAL PREP &
COOKING TIME:
25 MINS

BEEF & APRICOT BOLOGNESE ❄

2 tbsp olive oil
1 small onion – peeled, chopped
250g tinned plum tomatoes
30g dried apricots – finely chopped
150g lean beef mince
1 tsp minced garlic
Pinch of ground black pepper
½ tsp ground garam masala
¼ tsp ground turmeric
150ml water
1 tbsp tomato puree
½ tsp dried mixed herbs
50g grated carrot (about 1 medium carrot) – washed, peeled, grated
Freshly cooked pasta, to serve

Beef, an extremely nutritious meat, is an excellent source of a range of B vitamins, protein, zinc and iron. This is a great meal for all-round healthy growth.

Heat the oil in a saucepan on medium-low heat, add the onion and sauté for 3–4 minutes until soft and golden. While the onion is cooking, place the plum tomatoes and apricots in a blender (or use a handheld blender) and blend until smooth. Set aside.

Add the beef to the onion and fry, stirring and breaking up the mince to avoid lumps, until the beef is opaque. Remove any excess liquid then add the garlic, black pepper, garam masala and turmeric and cook for a few seconds. Pour in the blended tomato and apricot sauce with the water, stir in the tomato puree and mixed herbs, reduce the heat to low and simmer (covered) for 15 minutes.

Add the carrot, stir and add some extra water if needed. Simmer for a further 10 minutes until the mince and carrots are tender.

Serve on a bed of freshly cooked spaghetti, mash or chop as required, then watch your little one slurp away. Freeze the remaining sauce for another time.

MAKES
4 SMALL
SERVINGS

TOTAL PREP &
COOKING TIME:
25 MINS

MATTER (PEAS) KEEMA CURRY ❄

2 tbsp olive oil
1 onion – peeled, chopped
1 whole clove
1 small cinnamon stick
1 tsp minced ginger
1 tsp minced garlic
100g lean lamb, beef
    or chicken mince
200g tinned chopped
    tomatoes
½ tsp ground cumin
½ tsp ground coriander
Pinch of ground black
    pepper
¼ tsp ground turmeric
¼ tsp ground mild
    paprika
½ tbsp tomato puree
60g frozen peas
Roti (see page 134),
    to serve
Plain full-fat yogurt,
    to serve

A keema curry for baby with an excellent mixture of essential amino acids, the building blocks of protein, for healthy growth, starch for energy, and yummy bright green antioxidant peas.

Heat the oil in a saucepan on medium heat and add the onion, clove and cinnamon stick. Sauté until the onion is soft and golden, then add the ginger, garlic and sauté for a further few seconds. Add the mince and stir, breaking up the mince to avoid lumps.

Drain off excess liquid, then add the chopped tomatoes, cumin, coriander, black pepper, turmeric, paprika and tomato puree and sauté for a further minute. Reduce the heat to low, add a splash of water and simmer (covered) for up to 15 minutes, or until the mince is thoroughly cooked.

Once the mince is cooked, add the peas to the pan, stir, cover and simmer for 2–3 minutes until the peas are tender. Remove from the heat, then remove the clove and cinnamon stick and discard. Serve to baby warm, mashed if required, with roti (if she is old enough) and a dollop of plain yogurt or my Cucumber raita on page 152. Delicious!

MAKES
2 SMALL HOTPOTS
OR 4 SMALL SERVINGS

TOTAL PREP &
COOKING TIME:
1 HOUR 45 MINS

HEARTY LAMB HOTPOT

20g unsalted butter, plus
a little extra melted
butter for brushing

100g lean boneless lamb,
trimmed of excess fat
and cut into 1cm cubes

Plain flour, for sprinkling

Olive oil, for frying

1 shallot – peeled,
chopped

50g (1 medium) carrot –
peeled, washed, grated

¼ tsp minced garlic

Large pinch of ground
coriander

Large pinch of ground
cumin

80ml low-salt lamb stock

Sprig of thyme

1 white potato – washed,
peeled, cut into 5mm-
thick slices

Delicious and satisfying, this traditional meal originates from the north of England and is a source of iron, zinc and protein, as well as energy for your baby.

Preheat the oven to 170°C/340°F/gas mark 3½. Melt the butter in a frying pan and add the lamb and flour. Stir until the lamb pieces have browned, then remove and divide equally between two small ovenproof dishes.

Heat a little olive oil in the same frying pan then add the shallot and carrot and sauté until the shallot is soft and golden. Add the garlic, coriander and cumin and sauté for a further few seconds, then divide the mixture between the ovenproof dishes, adding 40ml stock to each dish. Finally, strip the leaves from the sprig of thyme and sprinkle over the two dishes.

Overlap the potato slices on top of the lamb mixture to form a cover for the stew underneath. Brush a little melted butter or oil over the potato slices, cover the dishes tightly with foil and place on the middle shelf of the oven. Cook for 1 hour, then remove the foil and cook for a further 30 minutes until the potatoes brown.

Remove from the oven and allow to cool before mashing the meal as necessary for baby. For older children serve with a side of cooked vegetables for a more filling meal.

MAKES
4 SMALL
SERVINGS

TOTAL PREP &
COOKING TIME:
1 HOUR 40 MINS

LAMB & ROOT VEGETABLE CASSEROLE ❄

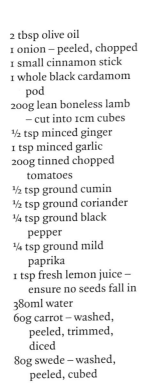

2 tbsp olive oil
1 onion – peeled, chopped
1 small cinnamon stick
1 whole black cardamom
   pod
200g lean boneless lamb
   – cut into 1cm cubes
½ tsp minced ginger
1 tsp minced garlic
200g tinned chopped
   tomatoes
½ tsp ground cumin
½ tsp ground coriander
¼ tsp ground black
   pepper
¼ tsp ground mild
   paprika
1 tsp fresh lemon juice –
   ensure no seeds fall in
380ml water
60g carrot – washed,
   peeled, trimmed,
   diced
80g swede – washed,
   peeled, cubed

This yummy slow-cooked casserole, with its beautiful blend of Indian spices, is packed with protein, vitamin C and iron, plus some beta-carotene.

Heat the oil in a saucepan on medium-low heat, add the onion, cinnamon stick and cardamom pod and sauté for 3–4 minutes. Add the lamb, ginger and garlic and cook for 5–6 minutes until the lamb is browned.

Add the chopped tomatoes, cumin, coriander, black pepper, paprika, lemon juice, water, carrot and swede to the pan, bring to the boil and simmer (covered) for 1 hour 25 minutes, or until the lamb is tender, stirring occasionally. If at any point the stew looks dry, add some extra water.

When the lamb is tender, remove and discard the cinnamon stick and cardamom pod. Mash or chop as required and serve to your little one warm with couscous or yummy mashed potato. For adults, serve with mash and a fresh salad.

MEAL PLAN 10–12 MONTHS

FROM 10 MONTHS	BREAKFAST	LUNCH	DINNER
MONDAY	Peanut butter and jam porridge	Cheesy tortilla slices	Saucy sardines
TUESDAY	Broccoli frittata with basil	Tropical jerk salmon	Curried lentils with squash
WEDNESDAY	Easy cheesy turmeric omelette	Orange Chicken Korma	Spicy spinach Roti Bites
THURSDAY	Plum chutney porridge	Curried lentils with squash	Matter (peas) keema curry with Cucumber raita
FRIDAY	Date and cinnamon eggy bread	Homemade dill fish fingers with lemon and herb dip	Mushroom and broccoli risotto
SATURDAY	Beetroot, apple and clove puree with full-fat Greek yogurt	Lamb and root vegetable casserole	Peri peri chicken strips with lemon and herb dip
SUNDAY	Banana and coconut pancakes	Beef and apricot bolognese	Thai chicken curry

Serve soft pieces of fruit or vegetables with every meal, along with water, formula or breastmilk to drink. For pudding, offer your little one full-fat Greek yogurt with a fruit puree of your choice.

STAGE 4:
BIG TABLE MEALS
(12 MONTHS TO GROWN-UP)

Congratulations! Your little one's taste buds have now blossomed into a beautiful, fragrant flower! The tiny flower bud that was closed a few months ago is no more – it has now flourished.

As you begin this chapter, your little one's flavour-led weaning journey will be complete. She has graduated on to the big family table, meaning you can all enjoy the same meals together (with some small changes for your little one). And the best bit... you don't need to cook separate meals any more!

The recipes in this chapter are adapted to be suitable for the whole family, without any added salt or chilli. Many of the dishes can be cooked whole, a small portion removed for your little one, then adults can add extra seasoning at the table. So everyone is happy!

READY FOR STAGE 4 FLAVOUR-LED WEANING CHECKLIST:

☐ 12 months of age

☐ Happily munching three balanced meals and two healthy snacks per day

☐ A few more teeth have surfaced

☐ Chewing is no longer an issue – the skill has been mastered

☐ All (or most) yummy flavour combinations have been accepted

☐ Little one is happily holding her spoon and is more in control when feeding herself

FLAVOUR

After completing stage 3 meals, baby now has a taste for real, adult-like home-cooked meals, so is ready to dive straight into this chapter. Her palate will also be well trained enough to accept new tastes and flavours, reducing the likelihood of a fussy eater emerging.

Keep experimenting with new flavours in meals and different cuisines long after you've finished the recipes in this chapter. There are endless flavour combinations: try adding a pinch of cayenne pepper, amchoor (mango powder) or Thai basil to everyday meals to alter the taste and keep meals interesting.

THE 'SMALL GROWN-UP'

Between the ages of 12 and 18 months, you'll notice your little one's motor skills will be further advanced, making her more independent. She'll be feeding herself with a spoon as well as using her hands. This newly found independence will also make her aware that she has a choice over what she eats, potentially causing mayhem at mealtimes. In this scenario I found family mealtimes were a great help! Toddlers learn new behaviour by imitating what parents, siblings and peers do, so family mealtimes encouraged Aaliyah to gobble up her meals, as she was eating the same as the rest us.

Setting Aaliyah's place at the dinner table also helped. It was great for making her feel recognised as a 'small grown-up' and an integral member of the family, which again encouraged her to eat her food.

MILK MILESTONE – COW'S MILK

From 12 months, milk feeds (now cow's milk) should be reduced to 300–350ml per day, as solids will now be her main source of nutrients. She will still need calcium, but can consume this from dairy produce such as cheese and yogurt. Excess milk consumption can mean babies are eating less solid food and missing out on key nutrients, such as iron.

Your little one is ready to drink cow's milk as a main milky drink, instead of formula. Cow's milk must be full-fat until the age of two. After that, provided your little one is a healthy weight, she can be moved onto semi-skimmed milk.

PORTION SIZES

With solids now your little one's main source of nutrients, below are portion sizes from the four main food groups to ensure your little one is receiving a healthy, well-balanced diet. See page 22 for examples of the types of foods that fall into each food group.

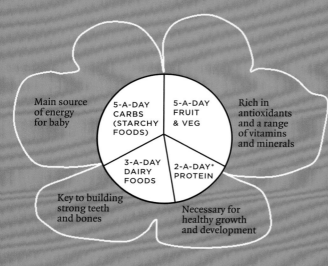

*3-a-day if baby is vegetarian

Adapted from the British Nutrition Foundation

APPETITE

Babies experience rapid growth within the first year, however when they reach toddlerhood their growth tends to slow down and the amount they eat will reflect this. So relax and don't be alarmed if your little one doesn't eat the full portion amount (above) every day. Appetites vary from baby to baby – it's perfectly normal. And remember, toddlers don't usually let themselves go hungry.

If you are concerned that your child isn't eating enough or eating a balanced diet, consult your GP.

FAMILY TIME

I love family mealtimes. It's a time to connect with one another, creating precious moments that should be enjoyed and cherished for years to come. So switch off the TV and enjoy your meals together.

SALT AND CHILLI

Recipes in this section include optional salt and chilli. Salt is not recommended for younger children and they may not be ready for chilli but I know people may wish to add it for older family members.

SERVES
A FAMILY
OF 4

TOTAL PREP &
COOKING TIME:
50 MINS

FAMILY AUBERGINE & COURGETTE BAKE

1 large aubergine –
   washed, trimmed, cut
   into 1cm-thick slices
1 large courgette –
   washed, trimmed, cut
   into 1cm-thick slices
1½ tbsp olive oil, plus
   extra for drizzling
1 onion – peeled, chopped
1½ tbsp minced garlic
2 tsp dried oregano
2 x 400g tins plum
   tomatoes, chopped
½ tsp ground black pepper
2 tsp ground mild paprika
Handful of fresh basil
   leaves – washed,
   roughly torn
Salt, to taste (optional)
Red chilli powder, to taste
   (optional)
30g Parmesan cheese
   (or vegetarian
   equivalent) – grated
80g dried breadcrumbs

~ TIP ~

Mature Cheddar cheese
is a great alternative to
Parmesan cheese in
this dish.

A lovely Italian dish. Just like a lasagne, but without
the pasta, this vegetable bake is easy to prepare and
delicious.

~~~~~~~~

Preheat the grill to medium-hot. Place the aubergine and
courgette slices on a grill rack and grill for 2–3 minutes
until the aubergine has browned and the courgette looks
a little crispy (it won't brown), then turn the slices over
and grill for a further 2–3 minutes to brown the other
side (you may need to do this in batches), then set aside.
Alternatively, grill them in batches in a dry griddle pan
(no oil).

While the vegetables are grilling, heat the olive oil in
a large non-stick frying pan, add the onion, garlic and
oregano and sauté for a few minutes until the onion is
golden. Add the tomatoes, black pepper and paprika
and simmer for 10–15 minutes. When the sauce has
reduced and thickened, add most of the basil (retaining
some for garnish) and stir. Remove a serving for your
little one and set aside, then add salt and chilli powder
(if using) to the main pan and stir. Preheat the oven
to 190°C/375°F/gas mark 5.

(recipe continued overleaf)

(recipe continued)

Spoon a thin layer of the sauce into the bottom of a rectangular or oval ovenproof dish, then scatter over most of the grated Parmesan. Add a layer of grilled aubergine and courgette slices (it doesn't matter if they overlap) and repeat the layering process with sauce, Parmesan and vegetables until all the ingredients are in the dish, retaining some of the vegetables and Parmesan for your little one's serving, which you can layer in a ramekin. Make sure the final layer is sauce. Scatter the main dish with a final sprinkle of Parmesan.

Toss the breadcrumbs in 2 teaspoons of olive oil and scatter them over the top of both bakes (the little one and the main serving), then sprinkle the remaining basil on top of both dishes and bake them on the middle shelf of the oven for 20–25 minutes until golden and bubbling. Remove from the oven and serve with a side of garlic bread, green salad or pasta salad.

SERVES
A FAMILY
OF 4 OR 5

TOTAL PREP &
COOKING TIME:
25 MINS

SIMPLE GARDEN VEGETABLE PAELLA

350g white basmati rice –
washed and drained
850ml hot low-salt
vegetable stock
1½ tsp ground turmeric
1 tbsp vegetable oil
Large pinch of saffron
strands
3 tbsp olive oil
3 tbsp minced garlic
1 tsp chilli flakes
(optional)
250g mushrooms –
washed, sliced
200g courgette –
trimmed, washed,
finely diced
150g frozen peas
½ tsp ground black
pepper
1 fresh lime
1 fresh lemon
handful of flat-leaf
parsley, chopped,
to garnish

**Yummy, sunny taste of Spain. This fragrant paella
always goes down well in my home. Great for energy,
and courgettes are a good source of fibre. Both rice
and courgettes provide a range of B vitamins.**

Place the rice in a large saucepan, pour in the stock,
add the turmeric, vegetable oil and saffron and stir.
Bring to the boil, then reduce the heat to low and simmer
(covered) for 10–12 minutes or until the rice is tender
and the water has been absorbed.

While the rice is cooking, heat the olive oil in a large
non-stick frying pan or wok. Toss in the garlic (and
chilli flakes, if using) and sauté for 1 min, then add the
mushrooms, courgette, peas, black pepper and a splash
of water. Sauté until the vegetables tender, then remove
from the heat and set aside.

Once the rice is cooked, transfer it to the frying pan
or wok with the vegetables, fluffing it up with a fork as
you go, and combine it with the vegetables. Cut the lime
in half and squeeze the juice from both halves onto the
paella, then stir gently. Sprinkle the parsley over the
paella, cut the lemon into wedges and place the wedges
on top of the paella to serve.

TOTAL PREP &
COOKING TIME:
1 HOUR 30 MINS

ROASTED VEGETABLE LASAGNE

2 aubergines – washed,
  pricked all over
Olive oil, for drizzling
  and frying
2 red peppers – washed,
  stems removed,
  deseeded, cut into
  large chunks
1 courgette – washed,
  trimmed, cut into
  1cm-thick slices
1 onion – peeled, chopped
1½ tbsp minced garlic
1 x 400g tin plum
  tomatoes – chopped
1 tbsp tomato puree
1 tbsp balsamic vinegar
5g fresh basil leaves,
  roughly torn
Salt, to taste (optional)
2 whole dried chillies –
  chopped (optional)
375g pack of no-pre-cook
  lasagne sheets
65g mature Cheddar
  cheese – grated

(continued overleaf)

There's no watery sauce sitting at the bottom of the dish with this winning veg lasagne! You could swap the vegetables here for sweet potato, fennel, yellow peppers and even some sundried tomatoes. Yum.

~~~~~~~~~

Preheat the oven to 200°C/400°F/gas mark 6. Place the aubergine on a baking tray, drizzle with a little olive oil and roast in the oven for 30–35 minutes. Add the peppers and courgette to the tray – drizzled with a little more oil – after the aubergine has been baking for 10 minutes. Once the aubergines begin to collapse and the peppers and courgettes begin to look tender and juicy, remove from the oven and leave to cool. Leave the oven on.

While the vegetables are roasting, make the herby white sauce. Melt the butter in a saucepan on low heat, then stir in the flour to form a paste (roux). Start pouring in the milk a little at a time, whisking vigorously. Once all the milk has been added, simmer until the sauce thickens, whisking occasionally to avoid lumps forming, then add the mixed herbs, black pepper, cheese and salt (if using) and stir to combine. Simmer until the sauce is thick enough to coat the back of your wooden spoon. Set aside.

(recipe continued overleaf)

Herby white sauce:
60g unsalted butter
60g plain flour
800ml whole or semi-
    skimmed milk
2 tsp dried mixed herbs
1 tsp ground black pepper
50g mature Cheddar
    cheese – grated
Salt, to taste (optional)

(recipe continued)

After the vegetables have cooled, cut the aubergines down the middle lengthways, scoop out the soft flesh, chop it up and set aside.

Heat 2 tablespoons of oil in a large non-stick frying pan, add the onion and cook until golden. Add the garlic, chopped aubergine, plum tomatoes (including the juice), tomato puree and balsamic vinegar. Break up the plum tomatoes with a wooden spoon until you no longer have any large lumps of tomato, then cook until the sauce reduces. When the sauce is almost ready tear the basil leaves and throw them into the sauce, along with the roasted red peppers and courgette. Combine well.

To make your little one's serving, place a layer of the vegetable sauce in the bottom of a small ramekin dish, add a lasagne sheet layer (you may need to break it to make it fit) and top with white sauce. Repeat the layers until the ramekin is full, ensuring the last layer is the herby white sauce. Top with a lovely layer of cheese (from the 65g) and set aside.

Add salt (if using) to the remaining herby white sauce, and add salt and dried chillies (if using) to the remaining vegetable sauce. Layer the vegetable sauce, lasagne sheets and white sauce in a family-sized rectangular ovenproof dish until the mixture has all been used up, using as many of the lasagne sheets as necessary and finishing with a layer of white sauce. Top with a layer of grated cheese and bake both dishes in the oven for 25–30 minutes until golden and bubbling. Serve with a side of garlic bread and some fresh salad.

SERVES
A FAMILY
OF 4

TOTAL PREP &
COOKING TIME:
1 HOUR

LEMONY SEA BASS WITH ROASTED VEGETABLES

4 x 90g boneless sea bass
   fillets – skin on
Salt, to taste (optional)

Marinade:
2 tbsp olive oil
2 tbsp minced garlic
Juice of 1 lemon – ensure
   no seeds fall in
Cracked black pepper,
   to taste

Roasted vegetables:
1kg baby potatoes –
   washed, skin on,
   cubed
4 red or yellow peppers
   – washed, deseeded,
   cut into big chunks
2 courgettes – washed,
   trimmed, sliced
Olive oil, for drizzling
Needles from 3 fresh
   rosemary sprigs,
   chopped

Sea bass is one of my absolute favourite fish. Especially served with juicy and crispy roasted vegetables. It is also an excellent quality protein.

Using a sharp knife, score the skin of the sea bass 2 or 3 times. This stops the fillets from curling in the pan as they cook. Set aside 1 sea bass fillet in a bowl for your little one, and place the remaining 3 fillets in a separate bowl, rubbing them with a little salt to taste on both sides.

Combine the marinade ingredients. Pour 1 tablespoon of the marinade over the fillet for your little one, and pour the remaining marinade over the remaining fillets – rub it into the fish well, cover and set aside to marinate while you prepare your veggies.

Preheat the oven to 200°C/400°F/gas mark 6. Lay the potatoes out on a baking tray, and the peppers and courgettes on another tray. Drizzle all the vegetables with olive oil and sprinkle evenly with the chopped rosemary. Use your hands to coat the vegetables with the rosemary

(recipe continued overleaf)

(recipe continued)

If you want to barbecue your sea bass, buy whole sea bass rather than fillets and marinate as above. It is easier to barbecue with skin on both sides.

and olive oil, then pop the trays into the oven and roast until tender and a little charred, tossing the veg halfway through. The potatoes will need 40–45 minutes in the oven, the peppers and courgettes will need 25–30 minutes.

About 5–10 minutes before your veggies are ready to come out of the oven, heat a little oil in a non-stick frying pan on medium-high heat.

Once the pan is hot, place the sea bass fillets in the pan, skin side down, and cook for 2–3 minutes to crisp the skin – do not move the fillet. When a brown crust begins to form around the edge of the fillet, flip the fillet over and cook for a further minute or two.

The sea bass is completely cooked when the flesh is white and flaky. Remove from the heat and serve immediately with the roasted vegetables. Feel free to season the vegetables at the table.

NO-FUSS TANDOORI FISH CURRY

2 tbsp olive oil
1½ tbsp minced garlic
1 x 400g tin plum tomatoes – chopped
2½ tbsp ground tandoori masala
2 tsp dark brown sugar
Juice of 1 lime
180g white potato (about 1 medium white potato) – washed, peeled, cubed
4 x 100g skinless and boneless white fish fillets, halved
Salt, to taste (optional)
Red chilli powder, to taste (optional)
Fresh coriander, to garnish – washed, chopped
Roti (see page 134) or rice, to serve

Tandoori masala is a fabulous spice blend. It includes all of your main spices, and a few extras, so is super charged with antioxidant and anti-inflammatory health benefits. The masala give the fish and potatoes a unique taste.

Heat the oil in a frying pan and add the garlic. Sauté for 1 minute then add the tomatoes, ground tandoori masala, sugar and lime juice. Cook the sauce for 6–8 minutes until it reduces and thickens.

While the sauce is simmering, steam the potato until tender, then set aside.

Once the sauce has reduced, add the fish fillets. Cover the fillets with the sauce and simmer on low heat for a few minutes until cooked through and flaky.

Once the fish is fully cooked, add the steamed potato to the curry and combine carefully with the sauce, trying not to break the fish pieces. Remove a serving for your baby and set aside. Stir salt and chilli powder (if using) into the main pan.

Finish off the main adult serving and your little one's serving with a sprinkle of coriander. Serve with roti or rice alongside my delicious Tomato dhal (see page 212).

MAKES
6 SKEWERS

TOTAL PREP &
COOKING TIME:
35 MINS

(PLUS OPTIONAL OVERNIGHT MARINATING TIME)

TAKEAWAY-STYLE CHICKEN TIKKA

2 skinless chicken breasts (about 500g) or boneless, skinless thighs – cut into large cubes

Marinade:
2 tbsp olive oil
3 tbsp tomato puree
1 tbsp fresh lemon juice – ensure no seeds fall in
1½ tbsp ground tandoori masala powder
Salt, to taste (optional)
Red chilli powder, to taste (optional)

Skewers:
1 yellow pepper – washed, deseeded, cut into large cubes
1 red pepper – washed, deseeded, cut into large cubes
1 red onion – peeled, cut into thick chunks

Naan bread, salad and Yogurt basil gravy (see page 198), to serve

This is perfect for a Saturday evening, or for a barbecue on a sunny summer's day. Packed with flavour and juicy vegetables, it tastes divine!

Soak 4 wooden skewers in cold water for 30 minutes.

To make the marinade, combine the oil, tomato puree, lemon juice and tandoori masala powder in a bowl. Take 1 tablespoon of the marinade and place it in another bowl for your little one. Add a few chicken pieces to the bowl, stir to coat and set aside. Add salt and chilli to the main marinade (if using) and pop in the remaining chicken. Stir to cover the chicken pieces and set aside to marinate while you prepare your veggies.

Thread a piece of chicken onto a wooden skewer and slide it to the bottom, following with a piece of pepper, then onion, repeating with chicken, pepper and onion until the skewer is full. Pop the skewer on a grill rack (with a tray underneath) and repeat the process until all of the chicken pieces and vegetables have been used up, and all the skewered kebabs are nicely lined up next to each other on the rack, remembering which skewer belongs to your little one!

If you can leave the chicken to marinate overnight, that would be ideal. The longer it marinates, the better the flavour.

Preheat the grill to medium and pop the skewers under the grill (or barbecue them), for 15–20 minutes, turning them over halfway through the cooking time. Keep an eye on them as you don't want to overcook the chicken (particularly if you're using breast meat, which can dry out quickly). Once the chicken is almost cooked, increase the heat of the grill slightly to get that lovely charred taste, if you like.

Serve the chicken skewers on naan bread with tons of fresh salad and my Yogurt basil gravy. For baby, the grilled chicken and vegetables will be more than enough. Offer her some Yogurt Basil gravy as a yummy dip, too.

SERVES
A FAMILY
OF 6

TOTAL PREP &
COOKING TIME:
4 HOURS

(PLUS 2 HOURS TO MARINATE)

AROMATIC ROAST CHICKEN

1.9kg whole chicken,
   giblets removed

Marinade:
4 tbsp olive oil
1½ tbsp minced garlic
1 tbsp minced ginger
2 tbsp tomato puree
1 tsp ground coriander
1 tsp ground turmeric
1½ tsp ground garam
   masala
1 tsp ground cumin
2½ tsp salt
Juice of 1 lemon
2 tsp red chilli powder
   (optional)

Yogurt Basil Gravy:
150g full-fat Greek yogurt
Handful of fresh basil
   leaves, roughly
   chopped
Handful of fresh mint
   leaves, roughly
   chopped
Freshly squeezed juice
   of ½ lime
3 tbsp milk
½ tsp granulated sugar
Salt, to taste (optional)

Here's a spicy twist on British roast, complete with yogurt basil gravy. Yum! Cut into strips, this roast chicken is a great finger food for your little one. Just remove the skin before serving, as this is where most of the salt and chilli powder will be.

Place all the ingredients for the marinade in a bowl and combine well. Smear the marinade all over the chicken. Set the chicken aside to marinate in the fridge for at least 2 hours, ideally overnight.

Preheat the oven to 180°C/350°F/gas mark 4. Place the chicken on a rack in a roasting tin, and place on the middle shelf of the oven. Roast for 1½ hours until the chicken is tender and the juices run clear when you pierce a thigh. Halfway through the cooking time, baste the chicken with the juices in the tin, and place a sheet of foil loosely over the top if it looks a little dry.

To make the gravy, place all of the ingredients in a food processor and blend until smooth.

Once the chicken is cooked, remove it from the oven and set it aside for a few minutes to rest before serving. Serve the chicken with the yogurt basil gravy and vegetables of your choice.

HEARTY CHICKEN, LEEK & MUSHROOM PIE

Pie filling:

2 tbsp olive oil

2 chicken breast fillets (skinless) – cut into cubes

1 tbsp minced garlic

1 large leek – washed, sliced into rings

400g mushrooms – washed, stems removed, caps sliced

Cracked black pepper, to taste

1 tsp dried chives

½ tsp ground garam masala

Red chilli powder or cayenne pepper, to taste (optional)

Sauce:

1 tbsp unsalted butter

2 tbsp plain flour

200ml hot low-salt chicken or vegetable stock

Pastry case:

1 sheet ready-rolled shortcrust pastry and 1 sheet ready-rolled puff pastry

1 egg, beaten

We Brits love a good pie. And wow! What a pie this is! I don't think I can use any more exclamation marks to make my point!! Creamy, hearty, filling and traditional, with a little spice for a twist on a British classic.

To make the pie filling, heat the oil in a large non-stick frying pan and add the chicken. Stir-fry the chicken for 2 minutes, then add the garlic, leek and mushrooms and stir-fry until the mushrooms have reduced in size. Add the black pepper, chives, garam masala and chilli powder or cayenne pepper (if using) and cook for a few more minutes. Set aside.

To make the sauce, melt the butter in a saucepan on low heat, then stir in the flour to form a paste (roux). Start pouring in the stock a little at a time, whisking vigorously to avoid any lumps forming. Once all the stock has been added, simmer until you have a lovely, creamy sauce. Remove from the heat, season to taste, add the pie filling to the sauce and stir gently. Allow to cool.

Preheat the oven to 200°C/400°F/gas mark 6 and brush the base (not the edges) of an ovenproof pie dish with oil. Lay the shortcrust pastry sheet in the dish. Gently

(recipe continued overleaf)

(recipe continued)

push the pastry into the sides of the dish, then press the pastry over the edge of the pie dish at the top. Prick the base with a fork, and blind bake the pastry for 15 minutes. (You can use baking beans if you have them, but it's not necessary.) Remove and set aside to cool, leaving the oven on.

Once cooled, roughly brush the bottom of the pastry case with egg wash (this helps avoid a soggy bottom) and pour in the pie filling. Place the puff pastry sheet on top to create the lid. Press the puff pastry edges firmly onto the edges of the dish and cut away the excess. Use a fork to press the pastry down and seal the edges.

Use the excess pastry to create a leaf decoration and stick the leaves onto the top with a little water.

Brush the top of the pie with more egg wash and bake in the oven for 25–30 minutes, until the top is golden brown. Remove from the oven and leave the pie to stand for a few minutes before serving. Serve with mash and roasted vegetables.

MAKES
6–7
BURGERS

TOTAL PREP &
COOKING TIME:
12 MINS

(PLUS 1 HOUR CHILL TIME)

JUICY BEEF BURGERS ❄

Burgers:
500g lean beef mince
1 small red onion – peeled,
    finely chopped
2 tsp minced garlic
1 tsp salt
¼ tsp ground black pepper
1 tsp dried sage
1 tsp Dijon mustard
1 egg
1 slice of day-old white
    bread – blended to
    form breadcrumbs
6–7 thin small slices of
    Cheddar cheese

To serve:
6–7 brioche burger
    buns, split
Tomato slices
Lettuce
Gherkins
Garlic mayo or sauce
    of choice

~ TIP ~

If making ahead of time,
you can freeze the burgers
by stacking them between
sheets of greaseproof paper
so they don't stick together.

Perfectly moist, delicious burgers with melted cheese in the centre. Protein and iron-rich, these are perfect as a substitute for a Saturday night takeaway.

Place all the ingredients for the burgers, except the cheese, in a bowl and combine well. Divide the seasoned mince into 6–7 equal-sized burgers, roll the mince into a ball with clean hands, then place each ball on a plate and flatten it. Fold a cheese slice in half and place on the right of each burger and fold the other side over so the mince patties resemble a half moon or calzone pizza. (This ensures the cheese is in the centre of the burger.) Reshape the burgers into a circle (no need to roll them into balls again) and press firmly with your hands to mould them into a burger shape.

Chill them in the fridge for 1 hour, then cook on the barbecue or in a griddle pan for 3–4 minutes on each side, or longer if you prefer the meat well done.

Serve the burgers in brioche burger buns topped with sliced tomatoes, lettuce, gherkins, garlic mayo or any other sauces of your choice. Sweet potato fries are lovely served alongside this yummy treat.

For baby, serve the burger on its own with the salad and sweet potato fries on the side.

CHINESE CASHEW CHICKEN

500g chicken breast fillets (skinless) – cut into cubes
1 tbsp cornflour
1 tbsp dark soy sauce
½ tsp ground black pepper
Salt, to taste (optional)
100g cashew nuts (crushed or chopped for young children)
2 tbsp flavourless oil
1½ tbsp minced ginger
3 spring onions – washed, cut into 2cm lengths
1 red or yellow pepper – washed, deseeded, sliced
1–2 tsp chilli flakes (optional)

Sauce:
1 tbsp dark soy sauce
2 tsp dark brown sugar
1 tsp cornflour

Cooked rice, to serve

Cashew nuts can be an allergen, so please be vigilant. Chop them into small pieces for children younger than five. If you are wary, simply leave out the cashews.

Place the chicken in a bowl with the cornflour, soy sauce, black pepper and salt (if using). Set aside and allow to marinate for 30 minutes.

While the chicken is marinating, toast the cashew nuts in a dry non-stick frying pan on medium-high heat until they begin to brown, then remove from the heat and set aside.

After the chicken has marinated for 30 minutes, heat the oil in a non-stick frying pan, add the chicken and stir-fry for 2 minutes. Add the ginger, spring onions, pepper and chilli flakes (if using) and stir-fry for a further 2–3 minutes.

Combine the sauce ingredients with 4 tablespoons of water and pour the sauce over the chicken and vegetables. Cook for a further 2–3 minutes until the chicken is cooked through and the sauce has thickened. Add the cashew nuts and combine well. Serve with rice.

SERVES
A FAMILY
OF 4

TOTAL PREP &
COOKING TIME:
1 HOUR 20 MINS

EASY CHEESY SHEPHERD'S PIE ❄

Pie filling:
50ml olive oil
500g lean lamb mince
1 onion – peeled, chopped
2 whole green cardamom
   pods, split
1 tbsp minced garlic
1 tbsp minced ginger
1 tbsp ground coriander
½ tbsp ground cumin
½ tsp ground black pepper
400ml low-salt lamb or
   vegetable stock
2 tbsp Worcestershire sauce
2 tbsp tomato puree
2 medium carrots –
   peeled, diced
Salt, to taste (optional)
Red chilli powder, to taste
   (optional)

Topping:
5 British red potatoes –
   washed, peeled, cubed
150ml whole milk
2 tbsp unsalted butter
¼ tsp ground black pepper
1 leek – cut into 1cm-thick
   slices
80g mature Cheddar cheese
   – grated

A lovely, satisfying meal that will go down well with the family. To get ahead, I like to prepare this on a Sunday, pop it in the fridge, and then freshly bake it one day during the week.

To make the pie filling, heat a little of the oil in a frying pan and add the lamb. Cook until browned, breaking up any lumps with a wooden spoon, then tip out any excess liquid.

While the mince is browning, heat the rest of the oil in a large saucepan, add the onion and cardamom pods and sauté until the onions are golden. Add the garlic, ginger, coriander, cumin and black pepper and sauté for a few seconds, then stir in the browned lamb mince.

Add the stock, Worcestershire sauce, tomato puree and carrots. Stir, bring to the boil and simmer (covered) on low heat for 40 minutes, until the sauce has reduced and thickened.

While the pie filling is cooking, place the potatoes in a large pan, cover with water, and boil until tender. Drain and mash. Then heat the milk with the butter in a

(recipe continued overleaf)

(recipe continued)

separate pan until melted and warm and add it to the mashed potatoes along with the black pepper. Combine until smooth and creamy and set aside.

Remove the cardamom pods from the filling mixture and leave the filling to cool before removing any excess oil from the surface.

Preheat the oven to 180°C/350°F/gas mark 4. Remove a serving of the filling mixture for your baby and place it in a ramekin dish. Top with some of the mashed potatoes and leek slices, sprinkle with a little grated Cheddar cheese (from the 80g) and set aside.

Add salt and red chilli powder (if using) to the pan of mince and stir. Spoon the cooled pie filling into a large ovenproof dish. Top with the remaining mashed potatoes and leeks and sprinkle with the remaining Cheddar cheese. Place both dishes in the oven and bake for 25–30 minutes until they begin to brown. Allow to cool before serving. This is delicious served alongside freshly steamed peas or a side salad.

SOUTH INDIAN-STYLE VEGETABLE CURRY

50ml olive oil
1 onion – peeled, chopped
½ tsp fennel seeds
1 tsp mustard seeds
4 whole cloves
4 whole black peppercorns
1 whole black cardamom pod
1 tbsp minced garlic
1 tbsp minced ginger
2 tomatoes, washed and chopped
½ tsp ground turmeric
1½ tsp ground cumin
1½ tsp ground coriander
400g tin light coconut milk (organic)
250g white mushrooms – washed, stems removed, caps cut into 3mm-thick slices
1 large courgette – washed, trimmed and diced
Juice of 1 lime
Salt, to taste
Red chilli powder, to taste
Fresh coriander, for garnish – washed, chopped

This creamy curry is packed with the goodness of fresh vegetables, including mushrooms and courgette. Mushrooms offer a deep flavour and are the 'meatiest' vegetables in terms of texture, which is why this curry works so well.

Heat the oil in a saucepan and add the onion, fennel seeds, mustard seeds, cloves, peppercorns and cardamom pod. Sauté for a few minutes to lightly cook the spices, then add the garlic, ginger, tomatoes, turmeric, cumin and ground coriander and cook until the tomatoes soften. Pour in the coconut milk, and simmer on low heat for 10–15 minutes.

While the sauce is cooking, pan-fry the mushrooms and courgette in a little extra olive oil for 5–6 minutes until the vegetables are tender. Once the sauce has finished cooking, add the vegetables to the sauce (including the water the vegetables released in the frying pan). Add the lime juice and combine well.

Remove a serving for your little one, then add salt and chillies to the main pot and stir. Garnish your serving and your little one's with coriander. Serve with cooked, fluffy basmati rice.

CHICKEN KOFTA CURRY ❄

Koftas:
500g lean chicken mince
2 tsp minced garlic
1½ tsp ground garam masala
1 tsp ground cumin
½ tsp ground turmeric
4 green chillies, pounded
1 tsp salt

Masala sauce:
50ml olive oil
1 onion – peeled, chopped
2 whole cloves
2 black peppercorns
2 cinnamon sticks
3 whole green cardamom pods – split
1 tbsp minced ginger
1 tbsp minced garlic
¼ tsp ground turmeric
1½ tsp ground cumin
1½ tsp ground coriander
1 tsp ground mild paprika
1 x 400g tin plum tomatoes
1½ tbsp plain yogurt, plus extra to serve
Salt, to taste (optional)
Red chilli powder, to taste (optional)

Fresh coriander, to garnish – washed, chopped
Roti (see page 134) or naan bread, to serve

Quick and flavoursome, this curry will satisfy every member of the family, including your little bundle of joy. You can make it with beef or lamb mince too.

Place the mince in a bowl then add the garlic and all of the ground spices and combine well. Remove 100g of the mixture for the baby's serving, roll into 1cm balls and set aside. Add the chillies and salt to the remaining mince and combine well. Roll into larger balls and set aside.

To make the sauce heat the oil in a large pan, add the onion, cloves, peppercorns, cinnamon sticks and cardamom and sauté on medium heat until the onions start to brown. Add the ginger, garlic and the remaining spices and sauté for a few seconds before adding the tomatoes and yogurt. Stir and cook the sauce for a few minutes, then reduce the heat to low and add all of the kofta balls. Simmer (covered) for 20–25 minutes, until the kofta are thoroughly cooked, stirring gently halfway through.

Once cooked, remove the small kofta balls along with some of the sauce and set aside (making sure there are no whole spices included in your little one's portion). Add salt and red chilli powder (if using) to the remaining sauce in the pan and stir. Garnish with coriander and serve with roti or naan and a dollop of yogurt.

SERVES
A FAMILY
OF 4

TOTAL PREP &
COOKING TIME:
35 MINS

TOMATO DHAL — PLAIN AND SIMPLE

2 tbsp olive oil
1 onion – peeled, chopped
1 tbsp minced garlic
1 tbsp minced ginger
Handful of fresh
    coriander, washed
    and roughly chopped,
    plus extra to garnish
1 tsp cumin seeds
1½ tsp ground coriander
½ tsp ground turmeric
200g tinned plum
    tomatoes, chopped
170g red lentils – soaked
    in cold water (10 mins),
    washed, drained
300ml water
Salt, to taste (optional)
2 tsp red chilli powder
    (optional)

Protein-rich, fibre-rich, simple and very delicious!

Heat the oil in a saucepan, add the onion, garlic, ginger, fresh coriander and cumin. Sauté for a few minutes until the onion is golden then add the ground coriander, turmeric and tomatoes and cook for 5–6 minutes until the tomatoes have reduced to make a concentrated masala.

Add the lentils and water, stir, bring to the boil, then reduce the heat to medium-low and simmer for 15–20 minutes until the lentils are tender and mushy. Once cooked, transfer the dhal to a food processor and blend until smooth (or use a handheld blender).

Remove a serving for your little one, and add salt and chilli powder (if using) to the adult serving. Garnish both servings with fresh coriander leaves and serve with rice or roti.

FLAVOUR INSPIRATION

The following table gives an over view of herb and spice combinations that work together, arranged by international types of cuisine. Most are safe for babies from 6 months. Some of the hotter spices, a little later.

FRENCH	Garlic Thyme Chervil	Nutmeg Dill Chives	Oregano Rosemary Fennel
BRITISH	Bay leaves Chives Thyme Nutmeg	Black pepper Parsley Cinnamon Mulled spices	Rosemary Sage Mint
INDIAN	Cumin Garlic Garam masala Cloves Chilli powder	Coriander seeds Ginger Paprika Cinnamon Cayenne pepper	Turmeric Cardamom Nutmeg Curry leaves Coriander
ITALIAN	Basil Garlic Bay leaves	Thyme Marjoram	Oregano Parsley
MEXICAN	Coriander Garlic powder Onion powder	Cumin Cinnamon Black pepper	Oregano Chilli powder Chipotle
CARIBBEAN	Allspice Ginger Bay leaves	Cloves Cinnamon Black pepper	Nutmeg Garlic Turmeric
THAI	Thai basil Cumin Cardamom Coriander seeds	Lemongrass Ginger Kaffir lime leaves Coriander	Garlic Turmeric Black pepper
MIDDLE-EASTERN	Cumin Cardamom Cloves Caraway seeds	Saffron Fenugreek seeds Star anise Garlic	Mint Parsley Za'atar Cinnamon
NORTH AFRICAN	Cardamom Cinnamon Paprika Ginger	Turmeric Clove Coriander Cumin	Nutmeg Black pepper Turmeric

NATURAL REMEDIES

Looking after your own little ray of sunshine is great fun, a LOT of hard work and challenging at times. Sleepless nights, teething pains, constipation, colds – the list goes on. I've had my fair share of challenges, and new ones continue to surface every day. Making natural homemade remedies is a life-saver!

If herbs and spices could talk, my guess is that not only would they be bragging about their multitude of rich flavours and tones, they'd also be showing off about their health benefits too. Ranging from supporting good immunity to offering teething-pain relief, easing digestion and more, herbs and spices really are the gold stars of the culinary class. Most spices are reputed to be antioxidant and anti-inflammatory, which protect us from infections, allergies, asthma and more.

Here's a handy reference guide showing you which herbs and spices I have found helpful with common ailments, and my recipes that use them in this book.

Please note, this is not a replacement for medical advice. If in doubt, you must always visit your doctor or health visitor.

· · · · ·

The best way to introduce herbs and spices into your diet is to use a combination in everyday cooking – your little one's meals and family meals. I find that their benefits are cumulative, building up gently over a period of time.

I remember Aaliyah was particularly unwell when she was teething. Her cheeks were flushed red, she was hot, dribbling and crying inconsolably! It was heart-breaking to see. I tried everything to ease her pain – medicines, teething toys, teething gels and teething granules. While the medicine brought down

AILMENT	HERBS AND SPICES			RECIPES
TEETHING PAIN	Cinnamon Black pepper	Nutmeg Cloves	Cardamom	Chewable teething sticks Gum-soothing squash
IMMUNE-BOOSTING (COLD/FLU PROTECTION)	Cinnamon Cumin Oregano Ginger Fennel seeds	Cardamom Turmeric Parsley Garlic	Cloves Black pepper Thyme Coriander seeds	beetroot and broccoli mash Mango and kiwi cold prevention
INDIGESTION	Coriander seeds Oregano Ginger Cinnamon Dill	Mint Cloves Turmeric Rosemary Nutmeg	Black pepper Cumin Cardamom Fennel seeds	Cauliflower and turmeric puree Kiwi, mint and lime puree
CONSTIPATION	Black pepper	Fenugreek seeds	Ginger	Tangy apple dhal Beetroot, apple and clove puree
DIARRHOEA	Cinnamon Saffron Nutmeg	Coriander seeds Cloves Thyme	Oregano	Banana and cinnamon puree
FLATULENCE (GAS)	Cardamom Ginger Fennel seeds Saffron	Cloves Dill Coriander seeds	Turmeric Rosemary Cumin	Calming cucumber puree
ANTI-BACTERIAL	Turmeric Oregano Basil	Paprika Ginger Dill	Cinnamon Fennel seeds Garlic	Beef and apricot bolognese Homemade dill fish fingers

ANTI-FUNGAL (NAPPY RASH PROTECTION)	Cloves Thyme	Cinnamon Garlic	Oregano	Tropical jerk salmon Lamb and root vegetable casserole
BRAIN-BOOSTING	Cloves Cinnamon Basil	Sage Coriander seeds Black pepper	Turmeric Rosemary	Strawberry, basil and banana puree
COUGHS	Thyme Cloves	Cardamom Black pepper	Ginger Dill	Apple and ginger puree
ASTHMA	Oregano Cardamom	Ginger	Saffron	Creamy masala salmon pasta
VOMITING/ NAUSEA	Cloves Coriander seeds	Oregano Saffron	Ginger Fennel seeds	Apple and ginger puree
SLEEP-INDUCING	Nutmeg	Saffron		Dreamy banana puree ZZZs sleepy cherry porridge

her fever, the other teething bits and pieces didn't seem to work quite as well. So in addition to these recommended aids, I created a yummy 'chewable teething stick' recipe (page 136) using cinnamon and nutmeg, which Aaliyah loved chewing on.

Nutmeg contains the compound eugenol, which is used as a natural medicine to treat toothache, and cinnamon contains pain-relieving compounds. If, like me, you are feeling helpless and running out of ideas to help soothe those uncomfortable symptoms, try adding some herbs and spices into your little one's meals. Or refer to the recipes in this book that I've created specifically to help with common parenting challenges.

USEFUL NOTES

ABBREVIATIONS	
g	gram
ml	millilitre
tbsp	tablespoon
tsp	teaspoon

All oven temperatures are for a conventional oven. If using a fan oven, set the temperature to 20°C lower than stated.

❄ All recipes marked with this symbol are freezer-friendly (see also page 31).

SPOON CONVERSIONS	
1 x UK teaspoon	5ml
1 x UK tablespoon	15ml (3 teaspoons)

LIQUID CONVERSIONS		
METRIC	IMPERIAL	CUPS
50ML	2fl oz	¼ cup
120ML	4fl oz	½ cup
175ML	6fl oz	¾ cup
250ML	8fl oz	1 cup

Please note all conversions are approximate.

INDEX

THANK YOU!

A lot of hard work has gone into this book and there are a few people I'd like to thank who helped me get there!

Team Ebury: A huge thank you to the excellent team at Ebury for helping me release such a brilliant book! My editor Laura Higginson, thank you for the direction from the very beginning, the book wouldn't be half as good were it not for your wonderful input. Also Laura Nickoll, Stephanie Evans, Lisa Footit and Lucy Harrison. Thank you all for your help and hard work on my book. Shantelle David and Kealey Rigden – thank you for your marketing and publicity support. Your assistance has been amazing. Rebecca Smart – thank you for believing in me and for giving me this opportunity. You've made my dreams come true.

Team Smith and Gilmour: Thank you for the outstanding design, and for visually bringing my book to life. It really is a wonderful looking book!

Team Ahmed: And finally, a VERY BIG thank you to my hubby Omar and my little princess Aaliyah for believing in me, and for putting up with me when I've been busy working away on my laptop on the weekends. I couldn't have written this book were it not for your continued support. You are both amazing! Keep the inspiration coming! Love you!

Thank you to the rest of my family for the continued support. X

10 9 8 7 6 5 4 3 2 1

Ebury Press, an imprint of Ebury Publishing,
20 Vauxhall Bridge Road,
London SW1V 2SA

Ebury Press is part of the Penguin Random House group of companies
whose addresses can be found at global.penguinrandomhouse.com

Penguin
Random House
UK

First published by Ebury Press in 2017

www.penguin.co.uk

A CIP catalogue record for this book is available from the British Library

ISBN 978 1 78503 346 9

Consultant Dietitian/Nutritionist: Fiona Hinton BSc, M Nut Diet, RD
Designed and typeset by Smith & Gilmour Ltd
Colour origination by Altaimage Ltd
Printed and bound in China by C&C Offset Printing Co., Ltd

MIX
Paper from
responsible sources
FSC® C018179

Penguin Random House is committed to a sustainable future for our
business, our readers and our planet. This book is made from Forest
Stewardship Council® certified paper.

Zainab is a mum to daughter Aaliyah, born in 2011, and the author of the award-winning cookbook *Easy Indian Super Meals*. She lives with her family in Leicester.

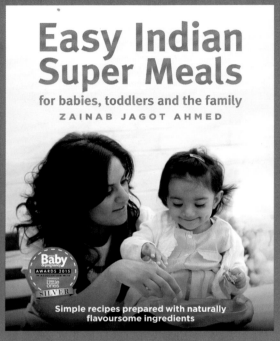

AVAILABLE NOW AT ALL GOOD BOOKSHOPS

FIND ZAINAB AT:
Website: www.zainabjagotahmed.com
Facebook: www.facebook.com/zainabjagotahmed
Twitter: @zainabjagahmed

Find out more about Zainab's flavour-led weaning method and get more help and support with your weaning experience at: www.flavourledweaning.com